ISO 21500 in Practice – .

Other publications by Van Haren Publishing

Van Haren Publishing (VHP) specializes in titles on Best Practices, methods and standards within four domains:

- IT and IT Management
- Architecture (Enterprise and IT)
- Business Management and
- Project Management

Van Haren Publishing offers a wide collection of whitepapers, templates, free e-books, trainer materials etc. in the **Van Haren Publishing Knowledge Base**: www.vanharen.net for more details.

Van Haren Publishing is also publishing on behalf of leading organizations and companies: ASLBiSL Foundation, CA, Centre Henri Tudor, Gaming Works, IACCM, IAOP, IPMA-NL, ITSqc, NAF, Ngi, PMI-NL, PON, The Open Group, The SOX Institute.

Topics are (per domain):

IT and IT Management

ABC of ICT
ASL®
CATS CM®
CMMI®
CoBIT
e-CF
Frameworx
ISO 17799
ISO 27001/27002
ISO 27002
ISO/IEC 20000
ISPL
IT Service CMM
ITIL®
MOF
MSF
SABSA

Architecture (Enterprise and IT)

ArchiMate®
GEA®
Novius Architectuur Methode
TOGAF®

Business Management

BiSL®
EFQM
eSCM
IACCM
ISA-95
ISO 9000/9001
OPBOK
SAP
SixSigma
SOX
SqEME®

Project, Program and Risk Management

A4-Projectmanagement
ICB / NCB
ISO 21500
MINCE®
M_o_R®
MSP™
P3O®
PMBOK® Guide
PRINCE2®

For the latest information on VHP publications, visit our website: www.vanharen.net.

ISO 21500 in Practice – A Management Guide

The International Guideline for Project Management

André Legerman
Anton Zandhuis
Gilbert Silvius
Rochelle Röber
Rommert Stellingwerf

Van Haren
PUBLISHING

Colophon

Title: ISO 21500 in Practice - A Management Guide
Subtitle: The International Guideline for Project Management
Series: Best Practice
Authors: André Legerman
Anton Zandhuis
Gilbert Silvius
Rochelle Röber
Rommert Stellingwerf

Text editor: Steve Newton
Publisher: Van Haren Publishing, Zaltbommel, www.vanharen.net
ISBN Hard copy: 978 90 8753 748 7
ISBN eBook: 978 90 8753 756 2
Edition: First edition, first impression, November 2013

Layout and DTP: CO2 Premedia, Amersfoort - NL

Contents

Foreword

The international guideline for project management, ISO 21500, was released in 2012 and has since been much talked about by the international community. Individuals and companies have been considering the subject matter in order to embrace, incorporate and/or adapt to the guidelines in ISO 21500 and much experience has been gained as a result.

This book is a revision of a publication in Dutch that was written at a time when ISO 21500 was still "new". This revised version, in English, therefore contains much of the solid practical content of its predecessor, but it also incorporates the complementary knowledge and experience gained since ISO 21500's release.

It not only features many tips on how to practically apply ISO 21500 in projects but it also takes a step backward and looks at the process of implementing ISO 21500 in an organization from the very beginning of interest at the bottom of the project management maturity scale to the point where benefits are being measured and continued improvement has become a sustainable process. In other words you see *how* to get the most value out of the guideline and how to make it work for you and your organization.

The arrival of ISO 21500 was a major milestone for the project management profession. It is the first real broad-based guideline for project management, and as such it will form the basis for current and future project management standards – in essence, a document that acts as a starting point for the further development of the project management profession. This was one of the key reasons for writing this book.

This book gives an answer to the most commonly asked questions about ISO 21500, with the central question: What is the importance of this guideline for the practice of project management?

The authors trust to give you, the project management professional, many tools and tips to get started with using the guideline and improving your project management skills and competences. Of course, now you have to take it from here, so we wish you the best of success and many new insights!

The translation team:
André Legerman
Anton Zandhuis
Gilbert Silvius
Rochelle Röber
Rommert Stellingwerf

1 Introduction

ISO 21500, officially published by the International Organization for Standardization (ISO) in September 2012, is a guideline for project management. It presents a common frame of reference and a process standard, that is intended to be overarching for all standards and concepts of project management. This international standard firmly positions projects within the context of programs and project portfolios, without extensively discussing the management of programs and project portfolios in depth.

1.1 WHY THIS BOOK

The objective of this book is to clarify ISO 21500. Guidance on project management is provided to show that it can be applied in virtually every type of organization, for both profit as well as non-profit organizations, and for every type of project, independent of complexity, size or duration.

1.2 WHO SHOULD READ THIS BOOK?

This book is aimed at everyone working in projects, sponsoring projects or those who will be using the outcomes of projects. In practice this logically includes everyone working in an organization. Projects are not limited to a specific branch or domain. A project is the most commonly applied organizational structure for realizing changes within, on behalf of, or between organizations.

The target audience of this book is, therefore, not limited to project managers and project team members. Of course, they form the primary audience for a guideline on project management. But the guideline is also relevant for line managers and other management functions in an organization. Especially since these functions are heavily impacted by projects and they can strongly influence and play an important part in the successful realization of a project. Therefore they can benefit from a generally accepted guideline on project management.

1.3 HOW TO READ THIS BOOK

This book describes the What, Why and How of ISO 21500 *Guidance on project management*, and it covers these aspects in that order.

Chapter 2 provides an introduction to the content of ISO 21500. It describes the background and the process that led to the creation of this standard. It also provides an overview of its structure and content, without literally copying its detailed contents. For the full unabridged version of the ISO Guideline for Project Management please go to (www.iso.org/iso/home/store.htm) or the website of your national ISO representative.

Chapter 3 explains the value of ISO 21500. In this chapter the Why of the standard is explained in more depth for the different roles in the organization and in the project environment.

Chapter 4 then continues by positioning the standard within the overall landscape of ISO standards and project management techniques, models and best practices. In this chapter we also highlight the views on this standard by the largest professional associations for the project management professions: PMI and IPMA. It will clarify how ISO 21500 relates to their publications, PMI's *A Guide to the Project Management Body of Knowledge* (*PMBOK® Guide*) and the *IPMA Competence Baseline* (ICB).

Chapter 5 deals with the implementation of ISO 21500 and its practical use in and by organizations.

In chapter 6 a roadmap is presented for the application of ISO 21500 to a project. This chapter also contains a case study, where a fictitious implementation scenario is presented as a practical example of how ISO 21500 can be applied.

Chapter 7 describes the expected future developments of the ISO standards in the domain of project, program and portfolio management and the impact on other standards and guides on project management. Is ISO 21500 the first step to a truly global standard on project management?

This book also aims to provide answers to the most important questions that the authors themselves had wondered about in relation to ISO 21500. Chapter 8 lists these questions, including clear references (where possible) to the applicable section in the book where this question is answered and discussed in more detail.

The Annexes contain information on the ISO organization and the international standardization process, as well as a list of specific terms and definitions as defined in the ISO 21500, together with various references. Finally, details of the authors of this book are provided.

In case you have any questions after reading this book, then please contact one of the authors. Based on this we can make improvements and add additional questions and answers and experiences to the next publication!

2 Origin and structure

This chapter describes the rationale for the creation of an ISO 21500 and the economic importance thereof. Subsequently, the history and the structure of the standard are briefly explained.

2.1 THE MOTIVATION FOR ISO 21500

In 2010, 18.6% of the Gross Domestic Product (GDP), or €15.9 trillion, was invested by the advanced economies (Australia, Belgium, Canada, Cyprus, Czech Republic, Denmark, Finland, France, Germany, Great Britain, Hong Kong, Iceland, Japan, Luxembourg, Netherlands, New Zealand, Norway, Portugal, San Marino, Taiwan, Sweden, Switzerland and United States). The expectation is that this will grow to 20.7% of the GDP, or €22.3 trillion, in 2016. To put these massive amounts in perspective: €8,600 is invested each year for each person from the newborns to senior citizens in the advanced economies. [1]

This is a huge amount. Certainly, with an investment of such a large sum of money, everyone would wish to see a return. Achieving a return on an investment indicates growth, and since the advent of the industrial revolution it is commonly accepted that a key condition for growth is standardization at the micro, middle and macro levels.

Many investments are managed in a project-based manner. Many of these projects and programs are staffed by various disciplines and externally hired co-workers. One expects that they all should cooperate effectively, that everyone should be able to perform their tasks well and at the same time, that all of this should be coordinated and implemented in a process-driven way.

For Information technology (IT) projects alone, there are at least seventeen different project management methods currently being used. One wonders who is capable of applying all of these methods correctly? What if the project is more complex than simply a pure IT project? How do you communicate with other stakeholders? Is anyone capable of understanding the whole picture? It is, therefore, time for a global guideline on how we can work together successfully in projects. ISO 21500 is a first step towards an overarching standard for the management of projects [2].

Although the role of ISO 21500 is limited in its reach, this guideline provides a good platform for the creation or further development of the project management methods in organizations. Proper control of the project management processes will increase the chances of project success.

An important feature of ISO 21500 is the introduction of a global standard and language for the field of project management. ISO 21500 is an overarching project management framework and reference point for the project practice of your own organization. If your practice conforms to the requirements and criteria of ISO 21500, then you have a sound basis for competent project managers to deliver good project results. In addition, you can show both internally in your organization, and externally, that you are able to deliver quality in your projects, because your project practice is based on the independent, internationally recognized benchmark for project management practice, namely ISO 21500. This guideline can have a direct, positive influence on the way that the projects are executed, and thereby indirectly enhance the quality of the project result.

2.2 TARGET AUDIENCE OF ISO 21500

The target audience of ISO 21500 includes:

- Senior managers and project sponsors, so that they gain a better understanding of the principles and practice of project management and therefore provide appropriate support and guidance to their project managers, project management teams, and the project teams;
- Project managers, project management teams, and project team members, so that they have a common base of comparison of their project standards and practices with those of others;

- Developers of national or organizational standards, for use in developing project management standards, which are consistent at a core level with those of others.[15]

Not explicitly mentioned in the standard, but no less relevant, are consultants, educators, coaches and trainers in the project management discipline. These also belong to the target audience, and they can therefore connect various generally known and bespoke project management methods, models and best practices to the ISO 21500 framework as a common frame of reference.

2.3 THE DEVELOPMENT OF ISO 21500

In 2006, the British Standards Institute (BSI), a member of ISO, took the initiative for an ISO guideline on project management by submitting a proposal for the development of an international guideline. With the forthcoming London Olympics (2012) it was determined that the national standard of the BSI needed to be revised.

The British proposal was supported by the U.S. representative within ISO and ANSI, after which it was sent out for ballot to the 164 countries that are connected to ISO to develop and publish standards. A majority of the ISO members voted positively on this proposal, and the development process was started.

2.3.1 Establishment of PC 236 and standards committees

In 2007, the ISO Project Committee (PC) 236 was set-up to develop the guideline for project management. Under the leadership of the initiating countries, the United Kingdom and the United States, over 100 subject matter experts from the 37 participating countries worked for several years to reach consensus on the concepts and processes that define project management. The experts represented national standards committees that were installed in the participating member countries to provide input from the professional communities in these countries.

In addition to the professional opinions of the subject matter experts, PC 236 also used market standards and references for project management as inputs to the development of the ISO 21500.

The two most important (international) professional associations for project management, the International Project Management Association (IPMA) and the Project Management Institute (PMI), both participated actively in the development of the project management guideline. IPMA was formally involved as a liaison to PC 236 and informally via IPMA representatives to the national standards committees. PMI acted as the secretary of PC 236 and was also informally involved via PMI representatives to the national standards committees. There was no formal representation of the UK Cabinet Office (responsible for the development of PRINCE2 until 1st January 2014).

2.3.2 Why this guideline?

The guideline has been developed to focus on a single project. More complex situations such as multi-projects and subprojects, are disregarded, however the guideline can also be effectively applied in these situations. This makes the guideline clear for all of the project's stakeholder groups. The members of that audience can easily relate their own role in projects to the guideline. ISO 21500 puts a strong emphasis on the involvement of the project environment, as this increases the chance that the project yields its expected added value.

ISO 21500 is a guideline for bridging differences and strengthening similarities in the way that people work together in projects. Often, many parties are involved in a project, including the project organization, the customer, fellow project managers, project co-workers, external providers, end users and/or the internal organization. ISO 21500 supports the communication between the parties involved by providing a uniform common language.

A common language is also essential in international and multi-disciplinary projects. In such projects the different teams often use varying methods, while cooperation is necessary. ISO 21500 can be a binding factor by relating the processes and deliverables of each method or methodology to the processes and deliverables of ISO 21500.

Existing sources that describe project management processes in more detail (such as PRINCE2 and the *PMBOK Guide*), provide more depth and support for the project manager when he runs a project. However, in order to involve parties that are not familiar with good project management methods, a compact and clear guideline is welcome.

2.3.3 Sources for ISO 21500

An international standard such as ISO 21500 has a broad target audience (see section 2.2) who use various references for project management. To ensure support for ISO 21500, it was imperative to define the core of project management concepts that is relevant to everyone. So, at the beginning of the development of ISO 21500, all of the national standards committees were given the opportunity to propose all the relevant sources of project management knowledge and best practices. These were general methods, national standards and existing ISO standards. A number of these sources were:

- The American ANSI standard (based on part of the *PMBOK Guide*, Third Edition);
- ICB version 3.0 (IPMA);
- PRINCE2 (UK Cabinet Office, from 1st January 2014 AXELOS, a Joint Venture between UK Government and Capita);
- The German DIN standard (DIN 69901 'Project Management: Project Management Systems');
- The BSI British Standard (BS6079 - 'BS ISO15188: 2001 – project management');
- ISO 9001 'Quality Management';
- ISO 10006 'Guidelines for quality management in projects';
- ISO 31000 'Risk Management - Principles and guidelines';
- IPMA: 'IPMA Competence Baseline version 3.0'.

ISO 21500 incorporated the competences that project co-workers should have in order to be able to contribute to the project as were listed in the ICB version 3.0:

- Technical: project management techniques;
- Behavioral: professional behavior of project personnel;
- Contextual: relations within the context of the project, i.e. both within and outside of the project environment.

2.3.4 The development process

ISO 21500 has been developed through a multi-stakeholder process involving experts from all over the world who have jointly determined what project management includes. During the development of an ISO standard, openness, transparency and consensus are key. It therefore takes some time to arrive at a common understanding of the content of a standard. This approach ensures that ISO guidelines can count on broad support.

The development process was mainly a repetition of a process that consists of two steps:
1. International meetings: discussing and writing texts and processing comments;
2. National standards committees: commenting on the texts and collecting feedback.

Between October 2007 and January 2012 six international meetings took place. During the first five meetings of five days, the participants worked on the text of ISO 21500. On the first days of each meeting the comments were processed and in the final days the text was updated. After the fifth meeting the draft of ISO 21500 was made available to the general public for comment. The sixth and final meeting lasted three days and was only focused on the processing of the final comments.

Hundreds of experts took part in the national standards committees, which together collected over a thousand comments per draft version. A comment must be provided with a justification for the proposed text change. The same eighty to a hundred delegates consistently attended these meetings and quickly became attuned to each other, resulting in an effective and dynamic international project team. As a result, the repetition of discussions was minimal and the guideline was completed within five years.

2.3.5 Involvement and contribution of the professional project management associations

As stated earlier, the professional associations PMI and IPMA participated actively in the development of ISO 21500.

In the structure and content of the guideline, the contribution of PMI is clearly visible. Although formulated at a more 'high level', the project management processes that ISO 21500 identifies, bear the signature of the process groups of the *PMBOK Guide*. In ISO 21500, the clause on processes is preceded by a clause on concepts that positions projects in the context of the value chain in organizations, where opportunities via the business case are converted into projects that create deliverables offering benefits to the organisation. The central position of the business case in projects is also found in PRINCE2. And although the PRINCE2 standard was not formally represented in the development process, the subject matter experts obviously paid reference to it.

The contribution of IPMA in ISO 21500 can, most explicitly, be found in the identification of project management competences that the guideline mentions:

- Technical: project management matters related to the deliverables of the project;
- Behavioral: the personal relationships in the project environment;
- Contextual: the relationship to management, both within and outside the project.

2.4 THE STRUCTURE

This section outlines the structure of ISO 21500. After the scope the structure of the document is briefly described.

2.4.1 The scope of ISO 21500

This international guideline describes project management and can be used by any type of organization, both profit and non-profit based; and for any type of project, regardless of complexity, size or duration.

It provides a high-level description of the concepts and processes that are generally accepted as constituting 'sound project management practices.' Although projects are viewed within the context of programs and project portfolios, this guideline does not go into the management of programs and project portfolios in any depth. Topics related to general management disciplines are only discussed if they have any bearing on the project management subject being discussed.

2.4.2 The structure of ISO 21500

The guideline is structured as follows:

- Clause 1 Scope;
- Clause 2 Terms and Definitions;
- Clause 3 Project Management Concepts;
- Clause 4 Project Management Processes;
- Annex A (Informative) Process group processes mapped to subject groups.

Annex A of ISO 21500 presents a graphical representation of the logical sequence of processes that one would go through during the course of a project.

In clause 1 the content and scope are described. See section 2.4.1.

In clause 2 sixteen project management terms and their definitions are listed, see Annex B in this book. The clause only defines those terms used in project management practice that are not adequately defined in either the current standard lists of ISO definitions or in the Oxford Dictionary.

Clause 3 describes key concepts that are specific for executing projects.

The following concepts are detailed:
- Project;
- Project management;
- Organizational strategy and projects;
- Project environment;
- Project governance;
- Projects and operations;
- Stakeholders and project organization;
- Competences of the project co-workers;
- Project life cycle;
- Project constraints;
- Relationship between project management concepts and processes.

Figure 2.1 shows the relationship between the project management concepts. The organizational strategy determines the opportunities. The opportunities are evaluated and must be determined. Selected opportunities are further developed in the business case or a similar document and may result in one or more projects with deliverables. Deliverables can be used to realize benefits. The benefits can serve as input to further develop the strategy of the organization.

Clause 4 identifies the recommended project management processes that should be applied to the entire project, to specific project phases, or to both.

The project management processes are suitable for projects in all organizations. Because projects require a high degree of coordination, it is necessary that each

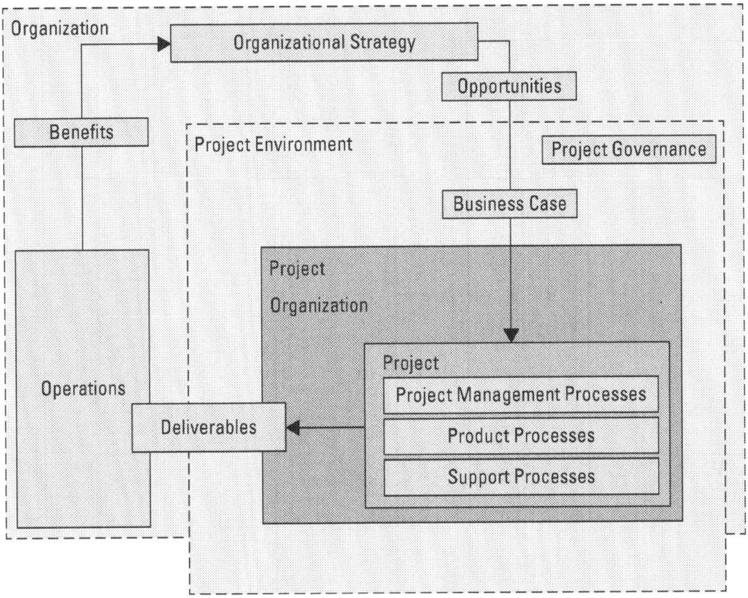

Legend:

- Boxes represent the project management concepts that are introduced in clause 3
- Arrows represent the logical order in which the concepts are connected to each other
- Dotted lines indicate the organizational limits

Figure 2.1 Overview of project management concepts and their relationship to each other (Source: BSI)

process used is properly aligned and linked to other processes to ensure the success of the project. One may need to repeat certain processes in order to define the requirements of stakeholders and fully comply with them, and to achieve agreement on the **project goals** (deliverables = what) and **project objectives** (business case = why).

The project management processes can be viewed from two perspectives: as process groups from the management view on a project, or as subject groups ('themes') from the perspective of grouping the processes by theme.

There are five process groups:

1. Initiation
2. Planning
3. Implementation

4. Controlling
5. Closing

and 39 processes, distributed among the following ten subject groups ('themes'):
1. Integration
2. Stakeholders
3. Scope
4. Resources
5. Time
6. Cost
7. Risk
8. Quality
9. Procurement
10. Communication

Within the processes, the activities that are carried out cover a particular aspect of managing a project. Examples are: 'Develop project plans' and 'Control costs'. All processes use inputs and result in outputs that, in turn, can be inputs for other processes. Inputs/outputs will generally consist of management documents, such as a contract, a project plan, a schedule or a progress report. Only the primary inputs/outputs are shown in ISO 21500.

The following is an example of process 26 'Develop the budget'.

Primary inputs	Primary outputs
• WBS • Cost estimate • Schedule • Project plans • Approved changes	• Budget

The processes are summarized in Table 2.1.

These processes need not be uniformly applied to all projects or all project phases. It is up to the project manager to determine what processes are appropriate and how strictly each process should be applied. In Annex A of ISO 21500 one can find a suggested flow of processes as applied to a project in execution.

Table 2.1 Summary of project management process groups and subject groups (Source: BSI)

Subject groups	Process groups				
	Initiating	Planning	Implementing	Controlling	Closing
Integration	4.3.2 Develop project charter	4.3.3 Develop project plans	4.3.4 Direct project work	4.3.5 Control project work 4.3.6 Control changes	4.3.7 Close project phase or project 4.3.8 Collect lessons learned
Stakeholder	4.3.9 Identify stakeholders		4.3.10 Manage stakeholders		
Scope		4.3.11 Define scope 4.3.12 Create work breakdown structure 4.3.13 Define activities		4.3.14 Control scope	
Resource	4.3.15 Establish project team	4.3.16 Estimate resources 4.3.17 Define project organization	4.3.18 Develop project team	4.3.19 Control resources 4.3.20 Manage project team	
Time		4.3.21 Sequence activities 4.3.22 Estimate activity durations 4.3.23 Develop schedule		4.3.24 Control schedule	
Cost		4.3.25 Estimate costs 4.3.26 Develop budget		4.3.27 Control costs	

Subject groups	Process groups				
	Initiating	Planning	Implementing	Controlling	Closing
Risk		4.3.28 Identify risks 4.3.29 Assess risks	4.3.30 Treat risks	4.3.31 Control risks	
Quality		4.3.32 Plan quality	4.3.33 Perform quality assurance	4.3.34 Perform quality control	
Procurement		4.3.35 Plan procurements	4.3.36 Select suppliers	4.3.37 Administer procurements	
Communication		4.3.38 Plan com-munications	4.3.39 Distribute information	4.3.40 Manage com-munications	

Figure 2.2 shows the interactions between the process groups and primary inputs and outputs in their logical context.

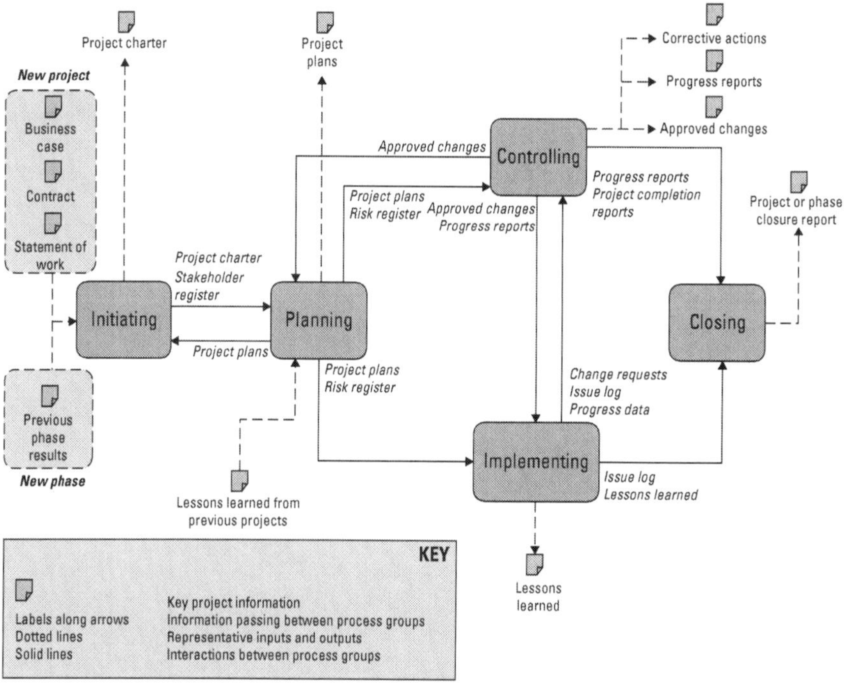

Figure 2.2 Process group interactions with the primary inputs and outputs (Source: BSI)

These process groups are based on the well known Deming Circle *(Plan-Do-Check-Act)* for continuous improvement, see figure 2.3.

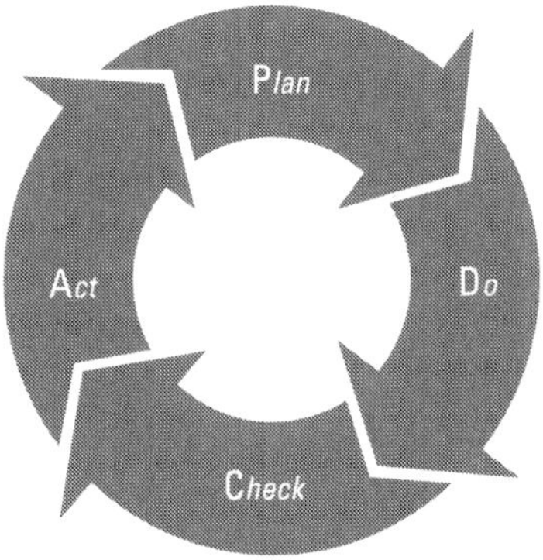

Figure 2.3 Deming Circle

3 Value of ISO 21500

This chapter answers the questions why and for whom ISO 21500 is important.

3.1 GENERAL IMPORTANCE

ISO guidelines and standards almost always get attention in relation to thinking and acting within companies and organizations. They are proven to add value in terms of communicating and organizing processes.

Standards and guidelines will never be exciting for most people. It's like a controller's audit, not exciting but necessary. They help to make things transparent and linkable. Thus far they are essential building blocks for improvement and innovation in our rapidly changing society. Standards and guidelines provide a foundation for trust. Therefore, a guideline for project management is also important for the project world.

ISO 21500 serves as an overarching reference for all methods, models and best practices of project management. The guideline also provides insight into the context of the project management discipline. The guideline contains clear descriptions of project management processes. These processes form a good basis for communication within and around projects, and help to clarify the responsibilities of all parties involved in a project.

ISO 21500 provides general principles for project management, which one can adapt to suit the project at hand or the company in which the project is executed.

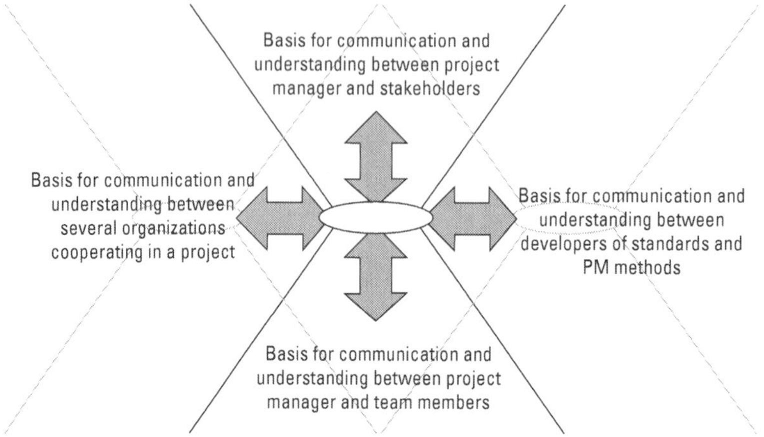

Figure 3.1 A binding factor in project management

ISO 21500 is, at this point in time, an informative standard without certification. It is not a project management method, such as PRINCE2. Because project management experts from more than thirty countries have been involved in developing ISO 21500, this guideline definitely has an international character and thus the potential to grow into a certifiable world standard.

Using ISO 21500 facilitates greater transparency, openness and involvement of the various stakeholders of a project. Because the framework is independently and unambiguously defined, the members of projects in which various organizations participate can work together efficiently on the basis of ISO 21500. ISO 21500 describes the processes and themes necessary for managing a project and the basic conditions that a project must satisfy. This will contribute to the successful initiation, implementation and completion of projects.

The guideline has been developed and is supported by most major project management organizations and can therefore count on a very broad acceptance. ISO 21500 is very significant for project management for the following reasons:

- ISO 21500 contains the generally accepted best practices that apply to all projects. This guideline is therefore a good starting point for shaping project management practice for an organization, or as a document that can be used as a reference to determine the maturity of project management within an organization.

- ISO 21500 is a globally accepted guideline for project management. In essence, this means a global project management language. By choosing ISO 21500 it will prevent any confusion that may arise between, for example, PRINCE2 and PMI proponents due to the fact that they use different definitions for the same project management products and activities. In addition, ISO 21500 makes communication between the international project team members in, for instance, virtual teams more efficient, because all participants work with the same definitions.
- The existence of so many project management methods increases the risk that you can get lost in the multitude of alternatives. ISO 21500 is an ideal starting point for all individuals involved in the initiation of projects such as project managers and sponsors. This is because it is a framework for project management and not a method. Once agreement has been reached on what will be done, based on the framework for a complete application of project management in a project, then you can look further at the methods, models, best practices and techniques that can be used to achieve these goals. You can use specific methods that are common in the work field in which the project is being carried out. And, of course, you can always refer back to the basic principles of ISO 21500.

What is the risk if you do not use ISO 21500? This presents both an opportunity and a threat. The opportunity is that you can demonstrate to your customers that you are actively engaged in the project management field and keeping abreast of the latest developments. The threat is that if you ignore ISO 21500 but the market demands it, you may lose market share. Alternatively, you may still have to take corrective measures to be able to show that your project management practice conforms to the principles of ISO 21500, which you may be unprepared for and which may add to your project costs.

3.2 VALUE FOR ORGANIZATIONS

3.2.1 Organizations in general

At first glance it may seem that the responsibility for ISO 21500 in an organization lies with the Project Management department or Project Management Office (PMO). One may reason that it is here where they understand projects and programs and ISO 21500 is indeed a guideline for project management.

However, the scope of a project, is usually well beyond that of the Project Management department or Project Management Office. Projects affect the regular business processes, the cash flow, the market, the available capacity and many more matters. The consequences of the introduction of new or revised products, services or results are noticeable both during the execution of the project and thereafter. In other words, projects affect the whole organization.

Since ISO 21500 is not a method but a collection of best practices, this guideline is a practical guide to help in describing the roles, responsibilities and processes in project management. It is also possible to check whether roles, responsibilities and processes are in compliance and to ensure that any noted deficiencies are resolved and improvements are made. In addition to the internal review of the organization's ability to meet its **own organizational requirements**, ISO 21500 can be used to assess whether the organization effectively complies with **external requirements,** such as those required by customers, legislation and regulations.

There are countless project management methods to choose from. Each has its own pros and cons. One can be very generic, whereas the other can be very specific. The advantage of a specific method is that it can be quite appropriate for the question at hand, but the downside is that it may not be quite as effective for other issues. Very generic methods, such as PRINCE2, have the advantage that they can be used for many different types of projects, however the downside is that they sometimes lack the necessary strength, because they are not specific enough or are too comprehensive.

A solution to this problem is to establish roles, responsibilities and processes for the project management practice in the organization. Then projects can be conducted uniformly irrespective of the method, model or adapted project management approach that is used by project teams. It must conform to these requirements and can be controlled and improved.

By anchoring ISO 21500 in the roles, responsibilities and processes of organizations, an organization can achieve maximum flexibility and freedom as to how they manage projects, while guaranteeing a reasonable degree of completeness in how project management is applied in their projects. Given the impact of projects in organizations this is not only desirable, but in most cases it is also necessary.

ISO 21500 even makes it possible to assess the practical translation of project management methods for use in the organization, as well as assuring the quality of the resultant project management processes.

3.2.2 Value for companies, governments and NGOs

All profit and non-profit organizations (companies, governments, non-governmental organizations (NGOs)) can make unambiguous arrangements if the parties work in accordance with this guideline. International enterprises and partnerships can use the guideline to align their projects and to efficiently manage their international suppliers.

ISO 21500 provides a common language and is therefore a reference when making decisions on the initiation and implementation of projects.

Applying ISO 21500 can bring many advantages to organizations that are involved in running projects:

- Consistency in the management of all projects;
- Possibility to develop a growth path for project management maturity in organizations;
- Stability in project organizations;
- Clarity and transparency through uniform procedures within projects;
- Tools for measuring and controlling projects, leading to more predictable projects;
- Better alignment between the sponsor and project organizations by clear process limits, assigning responsibilities and explicit rules for the conduct for ownership;
- General management tools and products such as a benchmark for good project governance;
- Standardization of project management within a company;
- Improved communication across organizational limits, despite applying different methods.

The project management products (such as project plans) are mentioned in generic terms in ISO 21500. No new words, abbreviations and terms are added, but the existing best practice terms that are common, are brought together. The use of these terms helps organizations to communicate with more focus and with a shared understanding of what is meant by a particular term.

Within all types of organizations the management of projects is focused on the same goal, i.e. the project deliverable. Therefore, there is, in principle, no difference whether ISO 21500 is applied in government organizations, NGOs or in the private sector. The varying purpose and nature of organizations will always bring about a difference in the practical interpretation and implementation of the guideline in specific organizational contexts.

When companies apply the guideline within their own organization, the following aspects may be important:

- The urge to achieve an ever shorter time-to-market period;
- The financial result, a short pay-back period;
- Risk management focused on potential (market) opportunities and threats;
- The efficient use of available budget.

Within the governmental sector an attempt will be made to connect organizational interests to the prevailing interests, such as:

- Public responsibility, susceptibility to fraud, obtaining broad support within and outside the organization;
- Risk management with a strong focus on security and reliability;
- Justified spending of public resources.

For NGOs as well as many other organizations a combination of these two perspectives will be applied. The guideline can have particular added value for international NGOs because of the simpler alignment of methods or practices.

3.2.3 Value for project management associations

Project management associations have many members, each with their own project management practice and their own stakeholders. With such a diversity of project practices and project participants, ISO 21500 is a good guideline for setting out clear arrangements. For instance, project management associations can use this guideline as an expression of transparency, to focus on quality improvement and to promote unambiguous arrangements in (international) production chains.

ISO 21500 can also contribute effectively to improving the communication within projects. Many communication problems are caused by misunderstandings about the meaning of basically simple processes and procedures, which in practice often prove to be more difficult. By putting arrangements in place that use a common language, this can be improved.

3.3 VALUE FOR SPECIFIC ROLES WITHIN AN ORGANIZATION

This section outlines the benefits of ISO 21500 for various roles that are assumed in projects. It shows how, in many cases, the different roles can benefit through the application of this guideline.

3.3.1 Value for the director/senior manager

Many business processes use standard methods and standard metrics like, for example, the decimal system for accounting. Due to the high degree of standardization in the field of accounting, new accountants become productive relatively quickly, because the general principles are already known. The same applies to product standards, for example for mobile communication facilities and social media. These were able to spread rapidly only because standards in this area had been developed and accepted.

ISO 21500 has been developed to ultimately create one common language for the project management profession. With a uniform set of definitions, concepts and processes it will indeed become simpler within organizations to manage the preparation, the communication, the direction, the control and the successful delivery of a project.

The same applies to the cooperation between organizations; as the cooperating partners comply with an objective external guideline, the alignment of project arrangements, product definitions, mutual responsibilities and the associated monitoring becomes a routine event and is not time consuming.

In short, in this way the director or senior manager can show that internally the business is in order or, if necessary, that there is a need to reorganize.

3.3.2 Value for the sponsor and members of the steering committee

Sponsors no longer need to prescribe that a particular method or practice should be used simply because they are familiar with them. They only need to demand that contractors use the terms, definitions, concepts and processes of ISO 21500.

If contractors are comfortable with their own methods or practices, they can continue to use these, under the condition that they adhere to the terms, definitions, concepts and processes of ISO 21500. These sponsors can also assess their own organizations or have it assessed to determine whether their own methods or practices in accordance with ISO 21500 and whether it validates his confidence in it as the best option for the management of the project.

3.3.3 Value for the quality manager

The ISO organization is known worldwide in the area of quality. The standards and guidelines of ISO are globally accepted and evaluated as a reference point for assurance of a certain base level of product quality and process quality.

An example is ISO 9001, the standard for quality management. Worldwide there are more than one million organizations certified against this standard [6]. In the normal business practice, customers increasingly use an ISO 9001 certification as the basic selection criterion for their suppliers.

ISO 21500 also pays attention to quality: see the subject group ('theme') Quality in the processes 'Plan quality' (section 3.4.32), 'Perform quality assurance' (section 3.4.33) and 'Perform quality control' (section 4.3.34). This means that the quality of the project deliverables within the project is assured. ISO 21500 provides links for integration with the concept of quality assurance within an organization.

3.3.4 Value for the contractor (supplier)

Contractors (suppliers) who run their project assignments in compliance with ISO 21500 can present themselves as a professional project management organization. The added value for both the contractor as the customers and sponsors is that specifying, adapting and delivering (intermediate) products can be organized in a transparent manner. This saves time and money during all phases of a project: from the start-up phase (shorter negotiations on procedures covering how to work together) to the deliverable (clear arrangements on quality assurance and quality transfer).

ISO 21500 can avoid the argument as to which method to apply. For example, when one hires external expertise or when one discusses models, methods and best practices, such as ICB, PRINCE2 and the *PMBOK Guide*. When the guideline has established itself sufficiently, contractors may assess their practices against the guideline. If their practices are aligned, they will more easily gain the trust of the sponsor.

3.3.5 Value for the project manager

With ISO 21500, project managers are able to check their own project management practice for completeness and consistency.

Because ISO 21500 is a guideline, it cannot be used formally for certification. It is simply a reference document. However, based on ISO 21500, the project manager can perform a self-reflection by asking the question: In my work as project manager, how do I deal with the terms, definitions, concepts, process groups, subject groups and processes of ISO 21500?

In addition, ISO 21500, as previously described, can serve as a communication means between project managers of different organizations that have to work together, however while using different project management methods. If all project managers have checked their method against ISO 21500, they can conveniently exchange information on the running of their projects.

Also, having knowledge of ISO 21500 and its application can yield extra points in the evaluation of their Curriculum Vitae, when project managers are being screened for an assignment or applying for a job. By taking good note of ISO 21500 a project manager is aware of the general best practices in the project management field and the international project management language. This allows project managers to act more effectively in their role.

3.3.6 Value for the project consultant and the members of the project department (PMO)

The project consultant generally supports more than one project within an organization. To fill the role of project consultant efficiently a certain degree of standardization is required in structuring projects. ISO 21500 provides a comprehensive, universally applicable set of definitions, concepts and project management processes. This set can be used to implement a project management practice in their own organization. The advantage is that projects across multiple organizations, for example in chain co-operation, can be managed more easily. Provided, of course, that the chain partners also conform to ISO 21500.

The PMO (Project Management Office) can assess and compare the common key principles and selected practice with peers. In addition, based on ISO 21500, the PMO can establish roles, responsibilities and processes, which can be audited easily and which are independent of specific methods and techniques.

3.3.7 Value for project team members

Projects are unique in nature and provide a unique product, service or result for an organization. Team members however, require the stability that comes from knowing what to expect and what is expected of them. This does not change from project to project, although the priority and urgency of these basic needs may vary.

Implementing ISO 21500 will reduce the risk that projects that are insufficiently planned and are managed under a great deal of stress with resultant overtime and a tense atmosphere lead to a 'successful outcome' at the expense of the co-workers. ISO 21500 emphasizes the 'knowing what to expect at the start'. This helps to ensure that the entire project team is adequately informed of the progress and flexibility in delivery dates. This is an important basic need of project co-workers: being informed.

When all aspects of the project are well planned, including the required staffing, clear communication and team involvement, as recommended by ISO 21500, then everyone in the team will know what is expected of him/her and what they can and may expect from each other. ISO 21500 describes the important aspects that are necessary for good teamwork and a healthy working atmosphere. The result is that the team works and communicates in a more efficient and coordinated way and promotes clear rules of conduct to quickly solve conflicts and misunderstandings.

When the basic environment is stable, the project team can bring the more high-risk tasks to a successful solution or to an acceptable outcome. The work environment is more relaxed if a project team has its house in order and the team members know how to deal with changes and problems. The structure promotes disciplined, professional behavior. Project team members experience security and stability if they are confident with a good, supportive system. This will make them feel free to direct all of their energy and power into the realization of the project objectives. This structure also ensures that processes are repeatable and the environment is reproducible for every project. This, in turn, helps to increase the levels of experience and competence for both the individuals and the organization.

3.3.8 Value for the program manager

ISO 21500 enables the program manager to standardize all projects that are part of the program. In addition, the program manager can more easily select and contract external parties by requiring them to prove that their project practices and deliverables conform to ISO 21500.

Furthermore, the program manager is able to more clearly map interdependencies between projects and manage these dependencies more efficiently by using ISO 21500 as the reference for the structuring, phasing, documenting and reporting of the projects.

3.3.9 Value for the portfolio manager

When it comes to developing and applying project portfolio standards and models, ISO 21500 can be used to describe individual projects in a structured way and as a reference framework for projects.

A difficult task for the portfolio manager is to advise on non-related projects and to monitor these during their lifetime. If, in addition, different methods are used to describe the projects, then they become difficult to compare in any way. ISO 21500 provides support to the project portfolio manager in these situations.

3.4 VALUE FOR CUSTOMERS AND USERS

When the project management practice has been designed in accordance with ISO 21500, the customer - who is the ultimate user of the project result - knows that the project will be carried out in line with generally accepted principles of good project management. This is an indication to the customer that the project manager has been educated in the profession.

Working in compliance with ISO 21500 not only means looking at customer requirements and the products that have to be delivered according to the contract. It also means that the project objectives are discussed with the customer, along with any threats or opportunities related to the achievement of those objectives. These are documented in the business case - one of the key products of ISO 21500 - which contains the justification for starting and continuing the project so that the right project outcome is delivered.

3.5 VALUE FOR MANY TYPES OF PROJECTS

A project consists of a set of processes comprising coordinated work activities with start and end dates. These work activities are carried out to realize the project objective(s).

Although projects may have many similarities, each project is in fact unique. The differences typically result from:

- Type of deliverable: a product, a service, a process or an outcome;
- Size;
- Number of stakeholders;
- Importance and influence of stakeholders;
- Resources and competences required;
- Constraints;
- How the processes are aligned with the deliverables.

ISO 21500 is applicable to any type of project. The guideline describes a project as a temporary organization. This is done deliberately since many of the principles associated with managing an organization also apply to the realization of a project.

The deliverables of the project can range from physical products (e.g. a new machine for a factory) to a service (e.g. training), a result (e.g. a new work method) or a combination thereof (e.g. a full implementation of a new Enterprise Resource Planning (ERP) system within an organization).

The concepts and processes of ISO 21500 are also applicable to a 'multi-stakeholder project', a project in which several parties are directly involved in the running and/or the results thereof. An example is the construction of public transport infrastructure (such as highways and railroads).

3.6 VALUE FOR EDUCATION AND RESEARCH

In terms of education and research, ISO 21500 provides a good starting point to continue to build on research projects and training programs. The (scientific) research in the field of projects is growing. Several thriving research centers around the world are engaged in project management. For international comparability and dissemination of the results of this research, it is important that a common framework of concepts and definitions exist. ISO 21500 provides this framework and is a widely accepted source for references in research and publications.

It also makes sense to use ISO 21500 as the starting point in education and training. The challenge here is bigger, however, because many courses in the area of project management are built around specific market guidelines and/or methods such as PRINCE2, *PMBOK Guide* and ICB. This is especially true in the private training market. The expectation is that these methods, models and best practices are going to conform to ISO 21500. Trainers should, therefore, look to include ISO 21500 in their training programs.

ISO 21500 offers a good initial exposure to project management for many technical and/or business management programs at secondary school, college and university levels. In-depth project management programs, such as those designed as minor and major subjects or master courses at some colleges and universities, can use ISO 21500 as foundational theory, and this may, for example, lead to further research projects.

4 Positioning ISO 21500 in the project management landscape

This chapter answers the question of whether the ISO 21500 is a directive guideline or a standard. The discussion continues by looking at the positioning of ISO 21500 in relation to other methods, models and approaches for project management that are out there, as well as to other ISO standards.

4.1 IS ISO 21500 A GUIDELINE OR STANDARD?[1]

A standard is a voluntary agreement among stakeholders about a product, service, result or process. The agreements are recorded in the form of terms and definitions, functional and performance oriented requirements, definitive procedures and best practices. One can also make a distinction between two types of standards: a standard with a descriptive (informative) character, and a standard with a prescriptive (normative) character.

When we talk about a **standard**, we usually mean the normative and prescriptive standard. When we talk about a descriptive and informational standard, then we are generally referring to a **guideline**.

A guideline specifies what is expected based on the generic requirements of goods, services, and personal attributes for a specific sector. A guideline does not explain precisely *how* one should go about meeting those requirements; rather it is a guide to **what should be done**. Standards are more prescriptive in that they specify **how things should be done**.

1 This paragraph hints at a possibility for the future. At the time this book was written though, there were initiatives to pilot a web based self-declaration ISO 21500.

ISO 21500 has been written as a guideline and it has not been specifically designed for, nor is it suitable for certification purposes. It is not a prescriptive document that mandates compliance, such as the standards ISO 9001 *Quality Management - Requirements* or ISO 14001 *Environmental Management Systems - Requirements with guidance for usage*. These standards stipulate requirements with which a company must comply in order for the organization's processes, or a particular aspect of its business process, to be controlled and improved.

The next version of the ISO 21500 *Guidance for Project Management*, or an implementation version of it (a Code of Practice) could possibly have a more prescriptive character. An example of this is the ISO guideline *ISO 27001 Information technology - Security techniques - Information security management systems - Requirements*, which was developed as a guideline and was then followed by an implementation guide, namely by the more prescriptive ISO 27002 *Code of practice for information security management controls*. The objectives and controls of this code of practice are intended to be implemented to meet the requirements identified by a risk assessment.

Perhaps at a later stage the option can be considered to allow for the certification of individuals and/or organizations in ISO 21500. Companies may however, choose to issue a self-declaration for ISO 21500 just as with the ISO 26000 *Guidance on Social Responsibility* in organizations. A self-declaration allows an organization to state that, based on a review that it has undertaken of its own project management systems, it has met all of the specified requirements of ISO 21500 and is fully compliant.

To meet the needs of corporate social responsibility (CSR) in the Netherlands, for example, the Netherlands Standardization Institute (NEN) standards committee for CSR Practice developed the NPR 9026 *Practice Guideline for Self-declaration NEN-ISO 26000*. This is not a certification, but organizations can use this to explain how they apply the principles and guidelines in ISO 26000. And they can then demonstrate that they are compliant by publishing a declaration on a central publication website, the Publishing Platform ISO 26000. In this way organizations can present their social responsibility performance in a location where all of their stakeholders can find it and see how socially responsible they are.

Self-declaration of project management compliance and performance could likewise be very useful for organizations that apply project management in their daily business. Tenders for projects often require that each supplier conforms to a particular project management method, so it is certainly conceivable that customers could require that their suppliers and contractors prove they are applying ISO 21500 as a project management framework in their projects in the near future.

4.2 ISO 21500 AND PROJECT MANAGEMENT METHODS

ISO 21500 provides basic principles and general guidelines for project management. So the question remains: How does ISO 21500 add value to existing project management methods, such as PRINCE2 and the *PMBOK Guide*?

ISO 21500 is not intended as yet another project management method, but rather as a set of globally recognized principles and best practices for the application project management to which all project management methods must comply.

This guideline is intended as a common conceptual framework linking the many existing project management methods that often differ by country, industry and even between organizations.

A project management method is a tool to make a complex project or a complicated project management system of processes easier to follow and understand.

It does this by means of a model which is, in essence, a simplification of the reality in which a project operates, thereby making it easier to identify, manage and control the interfaces between the project's processes and those of the organization. Note that the method or model doesn't in itself make the project more manageable or controllable, rather it allows for a clearer view of the processes and their interfaces with each other and with the processes and departments of the organization, all of which can support the project team's efforts to manage and control project progress.

Each model also has a number of basic conditions. If these conditions are not met, then the model cannot be applied to the project's situation, and the best recourse would then be to select another, more appropriate model to use.

The models also tend to have their own jargon. The advantage of this is that project team members are able to communicate quickly and easily with each other by using a single (mutually understood) word or term of reference. The disadvantage of this, however, becomes apparent when similar words and terms are given different meanings in different project management methods. This is often due to the differences in fundamental assumptions and imposed conditions inherent to the models that form the basis of these methods.

Due to the multi-domain nature of most projects, it is common to find that several different project management methods are used by (sub) projects within a program or portfolio. This is certainly the case when several domains (e.g. ICT or Construction) have already put their 'own' project management processes in place because their method fits so well with their specific type of work, or because it meets their specific needs. Actually, most methods have come into existence due to the need for practical support of a specific (management) process within a given context. Within that context the method works so well that it would seem wasteful not to use it.

ISO 21500 allows us to 'transcend project management methods' and to agree on mutual ways of working and to interpret the terms of these agreements in the same way. It is with this goal in mind that international experts in the field of project management came together to establish the ISO 21500. They explored and compared various methods, models and approaches for project management and their efforts led to the creation of a truly independent, global guideline for project management, with a broad support base, that can be used as a frame of reference for most (if not all) project management methods.

ISO 21500 is a global common reference framework for project management within which everyone is entitled to use his own method or approach.

4.3 ISO 21500 AND ISO 9001

ISO 9001 'Quality Management Systems - Requirements' is an international normative standard that specifies the requirements for the quality management system of an organization. The purpose of ISO 9001 is to increase customer satisfaction by demonstrating that an organization has applied quality processes that enable it to consistently produce products or services that meet the requirements of the customer and that are compliant with the applicable laws and regulations. This includes processes for continuous improvement of the quality management system. This is achieved through the use of verification (does it meet the specified requirements?) and validation (does it meet the customer's expectations?).

What sets ISO 9001 apart is that by focusing on the quality management system (by means of the quality control processes), the standard is able to guarantee a minimal level of quality in products or services in any type of organization (from medical care through to the production of cars) with reasonable certainty. In essence ISO 9001 is a collection of best practices focused on managing the quality of processes with the motto: 'If you follow the process, then you can be reasonably sure that the quality of the products is assured.'

Experience shows that you cannot guarantee the quality of the end result will meet the desired specifications just by strictly following a project management method, model or approach. This is certainly also true for projects managed on the basis of ISO 21500. This then, is the difference between ISO 21500 and the quality processes of ISO 9001 that do actually guarantee the quality of the products or end result.

ISO 21500 has many similarities to ISO 9001, but the key difference is that it focuses on the **project management processes** as opposed to focusing on the **product realization processes**. Simply put, if one adheres to ISO 21500, then you can significantly reduce the probability of project management failure and this, of course, increases the chances of total project success. ISO 21500 therefore provides a significant link to the management of quality within an organization.

4.4 ISO 21500 AND PROJECT MANAGEMENT MATURITY

Various concepts and models for project management maturity all identify having a clear and managed process, including associated terminology, as an aspect of maturity. ISO 21500 provides a good basis for this. Implementing ISO 21500 can, therefore, contribute to the growth of project management maturity of an organization.

Some well-known models for project management maturity are:
- OPM3 of PMI;
- IPMADELTA of IPMA;
- P3M3 of AXELOS (a Joint Venture between UK Government and Capita);
- CMMI from Carnegie Mellon University.

It is expected that these models will soon be highlighting points that they have in common with ISO 21500.

4.5 ISO 21500 AND THE INTERNATIONAL PROFESSIONAL PROJECT MANAGEMENT ORGANIZATIONS

4.5.1 ISO 21500 and the Project Management Institute (PMI)

In line with their contribution to the development process, PMI acknowledged ISO 21500 as a global project management standard and aligned the fifth edition of the *PMBOK Guide*, their standard on project management, to ISO 21500. The most notable addition in the *PMBOK Guide* Fifth Edition that should be credited to the ISO 21500 development is the positioning of 'project stakeholder management' as a 'knowledge area'.

It might be expected that PMI will follow a similar alignment policy for possible future ISO guidelines on program management and portfolio management.

4.5.2 ISO 21500 and the International Project Management Association (IPMA)

IPMA did not announce a formal reaction following the release of ISO 21500, but several member organizations reacted positively to the guideline. ISO 21500 makes the link to the IPMA Competence Baseline (ICB) by briefly mentioning the three main competence groups. These competences fit perfectly within the frame presented by ISO 21500, and therefore the risk of conflicts between the ISO 21500 and the ICB is minimal. However, it is expected that IPMA will also align its terminology to the concepts and glossary as described in ISO 21500 when it develops the ICB version 4 in the future.

5 Implementing ISO 21500 in an organization

Since managing a project is a practical endeavor, this chapter is dedicated to showing you how to implement ISO 21500 in your organization and the next chapter explains how to practically apply ISO 21500 in your projects.

Implement ISO 21500 or Apply ISO 21500?

Implementation is done in order to help an organization to ***adopt*** something new and integrate it into the existing situation - a new way of working, a new tool, a new application, etc. Example: to implement ISO 21500 would be to add it to the organization's policies, procedures and work instructions, to create and coach others in the use of supporting tools, techniques and templates, to help the organization to start using the new things and to continually improve on them to ensure that the organization has optimized the tools to be as efficient as possible. The focus is on an organization and the goal is to establish ISO 21500 as the new way of working in the organization.

Application is when one acts to practically ***use*** the new thing, in this case, the implemented way of working. Example: to apply ISO 21500 to a project would be to use the structure, processes, products, principles, etc. when executing a project. The focus is on the actual use in a project.

You can, therefore, implement a way of working without physically performing that work. When you are actually doing that work according to the new way of working then you are applying what was implemented.

So, when deciding what to do first or next after discovering the ISO 21500 guideline, this definition will help you to choose your course of action.

5.1 ISO 21500 A TYPICAL IMPLEMENTATION ROADMAP FOR AN ORGANIZATION

The following paragraphs explain the rationale for the recommended Implementation Roadmap - the intention of its design. Section 5.2 goes into the steps in more detail than is presented in these paragraphs.

Every organization is different. The suggested Implementation Roadmap is therefore generic in that it covers the main steps that should form the foundation of your implementation plan without going into too much detail – this should be organization and/or project specific anyway.

An organization has been defined as a social entity that is structured and managed in order to achieve the same goals. While structure and management towards the achievement of common goals may sound a lot like a definition of project management, ultimately the most important part of the definition of an organization lies in its social nature. Organizations are made up of people and people have social needs and expectations alongside their shared business and organizational goals. Any change in the way of doing things in an organization disturbs the equilibrium and people are affected by this change, whether directly or indirectly. It is useful, therefore, to firstly attempt to understand the needs and interests of the people before attempting to disturb that equilibrium.

This Implementation Roadmap recognizes that the project organizations are social entities as well. A project organization interacts with an external environment that is also populated by people. This interaction takes place through many different forms of communication. The roadmap therefore encourages communication and awareness. It also promotes pre-project social contact and information sharing in order to allow the people in an organization to understand and develop an affinity with the subject matter, namely the introduction of the ISO 21500 before confronting them with 'deadlines' for change.

The first and sixth steps (see figure 5.1 on page 42) are primarily concerned with communication and deal respectively with preparing the organization for change (step 1) and supporting the organization after impactful changes have been made over a relatively longer period of time than most project durations (step 6). Step 6 ensures that the benefits envisaged in step 1 are achieved and communicates the progress of benefits realization to the rest of the organization.

Steps 2 to 5 are core project steps, based on the Plan-Do-Check-Act cycle, mentioned earlier in this book. These steps are designed to be repeated in every phase of an implementation project, thus allowing for feedback to be considered and corrective actions to be taken where necessary.

Never skip step 1 when starting up a second implementation project to release yet more process changes, deliverables or functionality. Always re-check the initial assumptions and validate the initial requirements. The organization may have grown in insight and its needs and priorities may have changed to some degree since the first time that you followed step 1. This change may make or break your chances of a successful implementation, so take the time and spend the effort to re-connect with the stakeholders before launching the next project.

We recommend that when formally starting up the implementation project you apply the principles of ISO 21500 as described in Chapter 6 of this book.

5.2 THE IMPLEMENTATION CYCLE

The process of implementing ISO 21500 in your organization can be translated into an implementation cycle, see figure 5.1.

5.2.1 The Implementation Roadmap model

The Implementation Roadmap model consists of the following steps:

1. **AWARENESS** and communication to research and market ideas, and gain buy-in for a new implementation project.

2. **PLANNING** for short-term implementation goals (an implementation project or program of several releases), and long-term benefits management.

3. **INCREMENTAL IMPLEMENTATION** to introduce new concepts, tools and templates at a pace that the organization can handle by means of individual implementation projects, or an implementation program with staggered releases of deliverables and/or functionality.

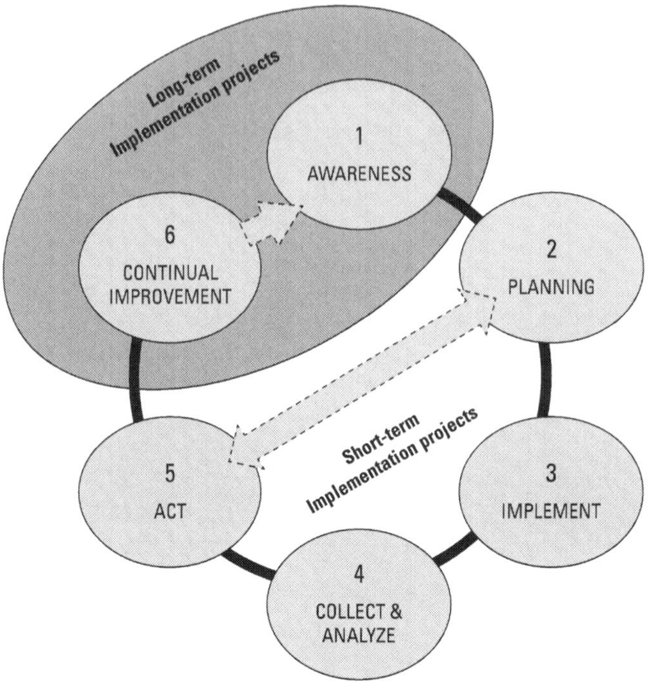

Figure 5.1 The implementation cycle

4. **COLLECTION & ANALYSIS** - during the implementation project or program you should collect metrics and feedback, analyze them and devise corrective actions.

5. **ACTION** - perform corrective actions as needed to keep the project on track and, where necessary, to adapt to the needs of the organization.

6. **CONTINUAL IMPROVEMENT** - after the hand-over of deliverables, continually track the benefits, and champion improvements to the newly implemented deliverables. Maintain communications - keep the organization aware of developments and successes in the implementation and derived benefits of using ISO 21500. This step may even lead to the initiation of new implementation projects and then you will be starting with step 1 again.

Back to 1: AWARENESS - when intending to introduce new concepts, tools, templates and so on, go back to the first step and do the research and communicative preparation necessary for the next new implementation.

5.2.2 The steps for implementation of ISO 21500

Step 1 AWARENESS, research and communication

1. Educate yourself and your team first. This book is a start but there are many articles, blogs and social media groups online that can help you with your own awareness of what ISO 21500 is and how it can be applied in project management practice.

Hints & Tips

In order to make the case for the implementation of ISO 21500 you need to be able to sell the concept to others. And, before you can sell the concept, you need to be sure of what it is and why your organization should want it.

- So do some research first. Learn how and where in project management practice (in what part of the management of a project) you would use the principles, products and concepts of ISO 21500.
- Then, develop a list of known organizational project problems or risks and list the ways that ISO 21500 can help with solving them.
- Develop a list of possible early adopters in your organization and approach them informally to chat about ISO 21500 as a possible solution to their needs.

None of the above requires a formal commitment of resources as yet, but you could be laying the groundwork for buy-in and support of a proposal for a formal implementation project.

2. Educate the organization on ISO 21500. (This could be the first step of your implementation project or could be a little project on its own.) Start with a long term informative campaign to create awareness and keep the organization up-to-date prior to implementation. There may be ramped up moments when the achievement of goals needs to be shared and celebrated with the organization and more subdued moments where information is provided in company media channels – on an intranet, company newsletter and posters for example.

3. Ensure that the internal Training department is informed and prepared to offer training and coaching on the application of ISO 21500.

Hints & Tips
Many organizations have an internal Training department or Training Officer. Tell them about ISO 21500, lend them a copy of this book and send them the links to articles that you have found interesting. This way they can become motivated to incorporate ISO 21500 into their project management training modules and coaching practice.

Step 2 PLANNING for implementation and beyond

1. Develop both a long term and a short tem plan for implementation. The Long Term Plan can focus on tracking the benefits, keeping the organization informed and introducing additional products such as tools, techniques and templates long after the initial implementation project has ended. Timeframes can range from one year to three years. These time frames are necessary for two main reasons:
   a. People need time to deal with change and to adopt new concepts. Give them the time they need and they will take it further in synergistic ways!
   b. The benefits only become evident AFTER the end of an implementation project and therefore there has to be a team that continues on for the long term to track, analyze, act, communicate and report on the success and benefits realized as a result of the implementation.

2. The Short Term Plan could be developed as an iterative project whereby short term goals are realized over shorter periods, from three weeks to per quarter. Don't flood the organization with too much change too soon. Each organization is different, so carefully consider what is achievable and the time needed (considering company culture, etc.) in order to realize it. Select a critical implementation element to start applying ISO 21500 on.

   Examples of short-term goals could be:
   a. Write a Project Management Glossary.
   b. Produce templates i.e. project charter templates, templates for Project Plans and Registers, and supporting instruction guides or work instructions.
   c. Develop a system for Change Control in projects including templates and conditions for change requests, submitting and processing them, including

the decision making process and timeframes that are applicable to your organization,
and so on.

Develop your short-term plan by choosing those goals that represent quick-wins for the organization. This immediately adds value and will help to increase buy-in and enthusiasm for what still has to follow in the implementation process.

3. Decide on what 'success' means for the organization and develop metrics to measure this success.

   Note: There is a difference between implementation success and the success of individual projects. This difference lies in the goals of each effort – the goals may differ in nature and tangible outcome, shape or form. For implementation it may mean signs of adoption of ISO 21500. For a project it may mean the successful outcome of an audit or the release of a deliverable. Be clear on what success is and to whom each goal or achieved objective matters. Plan for success. Also be aware that these definitions may change due to differing priorities and environmental change over the longer term – continually make sure that these definitions and metrics reflect the current expectations for each release or delivery moment.

   Examples of project success metrics are:
   a. First project charter in the new format;
   b. First meeting of the CCB.

   Examples of implementation (adoption of ISO 21500) success are:
   a. Percentage of new project charters in the new format;
   b. Appreciation of the change process;
   c. User/employee survey ratings.

   Identify specific information or metrics for the short term implementation project that will tell you how well your organization is adopting this practice. Ensure that the metrics are easy to collect because if they are time consuming and too complex to collect then people will lose interest and stop collecting them – so complex metrics and spreadsheets, etc will eventually provide no value. Rough measurements that are easy to collect usually provide sufficient information, and it is more likely that people will continue to collect them and the integrity of your reporting system will be maintained.

Step 3 INCREMENTAL IMPLEMENTATION

1. Implement ISO 21500 as planned. This could include the following phase goals:
   - All new projects structured according to ISO 21500 from date:......;
   - All new projects using a (company) standard list of management products by date:.......;
   - All process names, terms and definitions to be used in new projects started after date:....;

   And so on.

2. Pick a pilot project for the initial application of ISO 21500 (a company project other than the implementation projects themselves). Assist the project team as coach and mentor and eventual assessor as they go through all phases and apply the principles of ISO 21500 during the course of the project. Use the examples, hints and tips and case study contained in this guide as a starting point for the application of ISO 21500. Share and celebrate successes with the rest of the organization so that they are included in the journey and can grow with the project team.

Step 4 COLLECTION & ANALYSIS - gather metrics and analyze them.

1. Gather the metrics for success that you defined during planning.

2. Evaluate the implementation based on the objectives and metrics that you defined. Analyze them to identify any important constraints or additional requirements in your organization. These constraints could arise due to various types of issues or the increased risk of a particular problem becoming a reality.

Step 5 ACTION - perform corrective actions

1. Develop an action plan that focusses on elevating and solving or monitoring these constraints and/or realizing these important requirements.

2. Make adjustments based on your evaluation. Eliminate tools or templates that do not prove effective, and encourage the use of practices that are efficient and improve quality.

3. Determine the next step in implementation. Go back to 'Step 2 Planning' to bring the project back on track. Repeat this cycle for monitoring and control until the implementation project has been completed.

Step 6 CONTINUOUS IMPROVEMENT

1. Continue to examine how the adoption and use of ISO 21500 is going and track the growth in maturity of this implementation in the organization over a long period of time – say one to three years for a medium to large organization.

2. Document the trends.

3. Document the lessons learned.

4. Establish a **benefits team** that can meet every quarter of the year to reflect on post-implementation observations and the results gathered in the period. Members can individually champion ISO 21500 in their departments or domains and then they can report back to the group to generate insight and discussion about further improvements that can be incrementally applied to the organization's project management practice.

5. Continue to improve by supporting new project teams, training new employees to be aware of ISO 21500 and to apply ISO 21500 in their projects.

Step 1-repeat AWARENESS and continued communication

1. Repeat the cycle by keeping the organization informed on implementation progress and benefits realized post-implementation.

2. Offer tips, new insights and new tools, techniques and templates as they become available and communicate these in company media so that everyone knows that ISO 21500 is continually being improved.

3. Report on the success of long term goals and benefits achieved to management so that ROI (Return On Investment) and TCQ (Total Cost of Quality) can be considered and celebrated.

The result of a successful **implementation** of ISO 21500 is the actual use and application of the good practices that it offers. Chapter 6 will show how you can **apply** ISO 21500 to a project.

6 Applying ISO 21500 to projects

Since managing a project is a practical endeavor, this chapter is dedicated to showing you how to practically apply ISO 21500 to your projects and it concludes with a case study.

6.1 ISO 21500, A TYPICAL APPLICATION ROADMAP FOR A PROJECT

The elementary questions that every project manager should ask when starting up a project (why, who, what, when, where, how, how much, etc.) are covered by means of a step-by-step project roadmap which will illustrate how to apply the theory contained in the guideline. A fictitious case study is presented at the end of this chapter in order to further demonstrate these steps and to show you that the ISO 21500 can be directly applied in any project.

There is no 'magic bullet' to achieving project success. This is due to the fact that there is no single, standard approach to projects. It is for this reason that the roadmap outlined here does not assume to be anything more than a suggestion to show project managers how to start up, implement and close-out a project in a simple manner. It makes no claim to being a complete version of all of the process steps contained in the ISO 21500 Guideline, nor does it absolve the project manager from the responsibility for considering all of the factors of influence that are relevant to the project in a given situation when deciding on the most appropriate project management approach in order to achieve project success.

This roadmap is based on the ISO 21500 *Guideline for Project Management*. The ISO 21500 Guideline contains many more detailed process-steps that collectively form the basis for setting up a project. Along with a short explanation of each step you will also find information boxes containing useful hints and tips that can be used when applying ISO 21500 in your project.

6.2 ISO 21500 PROJECT APPLICATION ROADMAP

The ISO 21500 Project Application Roadmap consists of ten steps. These are shown in figure 6.

Note: between parentheses are references to the corresponding processes in the guideline, see Table 2.1.

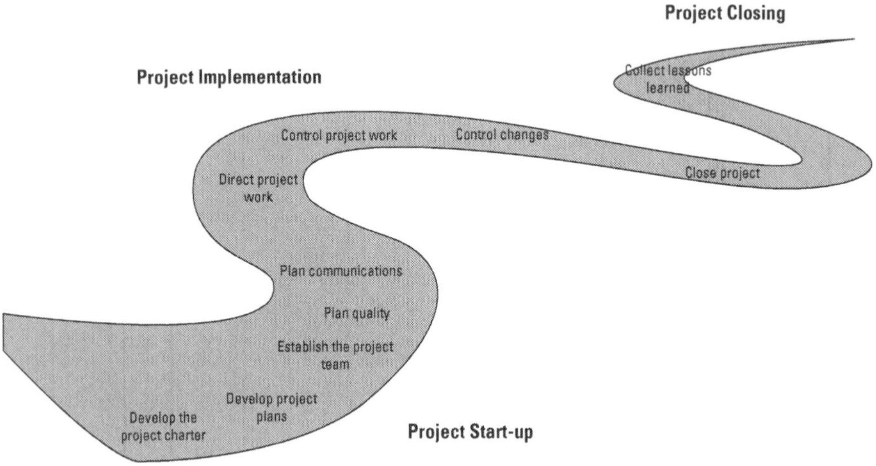

Figure 6.1 ISO 21500 Project Application Roadmap

Project Start-up

Step 1 Develop the project charter using a business case as input (4.3.2)

Step 2 Develop project plans, including detailed phase plans (4.3.3)

Step 3 Establish the project team (4.3.15)

Step 4 Plan quality (4.3.32)

Step 5 Plan communications (4.3.38)

Project Implementation

Step 6 Direct project work (4.3.4)

Step 7 Control project work (4.3.5)

Step 8 Control changes (4.3.6)

Project Closing

Step 9 Close project phase or project (4.3.7)

Step 10 Collect lessons learned (4.3.8)

Step 1 Develop the project charter (4.3.2)

Developing the project charter is the first and most important step in starting up a project. This is because it formally authorizes the project or a new project phase. It defines the responsibilities and authority of the project manager based on the business case.

Prior to starting up a project, the organization justifies the need for the project by means of a business case, thereby answering the **'WHY?'** question for the deliverables (products) that will be created by means of the project.

The business case links the project to the (strategic) objectives of the enterprise ensuring that the project remains aligned with the goals and interests of the primary stakeholder, the customer.

Hints & Tips

When deciding how to apply the ISO 21500 in a project, there are several options to choose from.

The guideline can be used as:

- A basis for applying project management principles during the execution of the whole project.
- A basis for project management quality assurance (for example as input into the structure of a checklist or audit, or as a maturity model to gauge the level of project management maturity that is evident) especially when a new project management method has been chosen and one wants to ensure that the right things are being done and the correct decisions have been made.
- As a basis for structuring project management processes for optimal alignment with the processes of the rest of the enterprise.

Step 2 Develop project plans

In this step the backbone of the project is established. Plans are the most important communication tools in any project. They give the project direction and make project control possible. The questions answered by performing this project management process are: WHO, WHAT, WHEN, WHERE, HOW and HOW MUCH?

Plans are where the solution and the means to achieve it are presented in clear detail, along with information on how much it will cost and the timelines involved.

Hints & Tips

The documents often involved in the application of ISO 21500 in a project could include the following, depending on the context and area of application:

- Policy documentation for the use and application of ISO 21500;
- Process descriptions;
- Templates;
- Checklists for reviews;
- A list containing organizational requirements (for the practical application of a project management guideline);
- Applicable lessons learned from previous projects.

The process of applying the ISO 21500 is an important experiential learning process for everyone involved. It is recommended that the full set of processes and their prescribed input and output documentation are used during this process. Only then can one discern which processes and documents are a good fit for the project within the organizational environment and context that it operates in. And only then can the true measure of added value be ascertained.

Note: Due to the fact that the ISO 21500 has only recently been released, there are no standard project management templates available as yet. As a result you will need to develop your own tailor-made templates.

Step 3 Establish project team

This is a crucial step in starting up a project – project work is primarily performed by people. So it is therefore not surprising that a great deal of past project success has been attributed to the people who made it happen.

In this step the project manager attempts to acquire persons with all (or most) of the necessary skill sets and competences for his team. Also, the team structure is determined, and roles and responsibilities are defined and assigned. These arrangements are an important step towards establishing effective communications within the project.

Hints & Tips
When implementing the ISO 21500 (as with the implementation of any other change in an organization) it is important to ensure the active involvement of people. These people in turn can become the champions of the application of ISO 21500 within the organization, thereby engendering the support necessary for the adoption of ISO 21500 by the organization, and ensuring the continued use of the newly created tools.

It may be useful to consider John Kotter's eight-step process to leading change in order to broaden the scope of your ISO 21500 implementation efforts and to set up further actions for implementation. The recommendation above will, for example, greatly complement Kotter's fifth step by empowering people to proactively help the change move forward.

Step 4 Plan quality (4.3.32)

It is necessary to start planning quality at the beginning of the project and to continue it throughout the project so that project efforts are always focused on answering the following question: "Are we delivering what the customer and the users require and expect?"

The project manager should determine whether the organization has its own (quality) standards that should be applied to the project. Compliance with these will prevent the realization of products that are deemed to be 'sub-standard' and therefore unacceptable by the users of those products and those responsible for acceptance testing.

Hints & Tips
In this step you determine which quality requirements apply to the products being made before the work gets underway to build them. This includes:

- Requirements for product quality (specifications);
- Requirements for product descriptions and how those descriptions are to be delivered (for example that all process diagrams should be formatted in the in-house company style and delivered in a certain software format.)
- Skills and competence requirements of the staff responsible for delivering products of an acceptable quality (e.g. minimal knowledge of specific quality standards, production methods, etc.)
- The manner by which products are produced (factored in inspection, quality assurance)

Step 5 Plan communications (4.3.38)
It always important to determine the communication needs of both the internal and the external stakeholders (that were identified in process 4.3.9 Identify Stakeholders, see Table 2.1). Everyone with an interest in a project has the potential to influence the results of the project, whether in a negative or a positive way. Choices have to be made as to whether the stakeholder should be actively involved in the execution of the project or whether passive forms of communication (e.g. a newsletter) would be sufficient. It is therefore wise to be aware of the following with regard to communicating with stakeholders:

- Type of information/relevance to their interest;
- Level of detail;
- Means of information delivery;
- Means of communicative involvement;
- Frequency of communications.

This is a non-exhaustive list. Please note that this step should be undertaken early on in the project, especially after a detailed analysis of the impacts and needs of stakeholders has been made, so that communications can be tailored to these needs. Effective communication is crucial to the success of the project.

Step 6 Direct project work (4.3.4)
Every project manager is expected to direct the performance of the planned activities. This will require that he/she manages the technical, administrative and organizational interfaces within the project. The project manager must see to it that all work carried out by the project team is properly coordinated so that the team members are working in alignment with each other, thereby ensuring that the products that were agreed upon are delivered. The success of the project will depend on how the project manager uses his/her leadership qualities to motivate the team and manage expectations.

Step 7 Control project work (4.3.5)
A project manager should not only coordinate the project activities, but also check, measure and evaluate them. This means that the project manager ensures all activities ultimately lead to a result. This gives the project a real and current picture of progress by showing what was done, what still needs to be done and how this information relates to expectations regarding time, budget, quality and scope. A major advantage of performing monitoring and control activities is that

improvements can actually be implemented within the project when it becomes clear that they are necessary in order to achieve the project's objectives.

Hints & Tips

Every well run project has someone to monitor and control project progress. When deciding **who** will do it, (and **how**), one first has to be clear on **what** precisely needs to be done. The requirement for progress information must be defined at the start of the project so that measurements and actions can be carried out consistently from the start to the end of the project.

One of the things that should be defined with regard to progress monitoring and control is which dimensions of progress reporting will be done, how and by whom. These dimensions include the following:

- **Costs** – setting up and monitoring the budget, cost plans for phases, etc.;
- **Time** – determining deadlines and main milestones, deciding on the best manageable level of granularity for setting up a project schedule;
- **Scope** – starting with the WBS and PBS (Product Breakdown Structures), you should keep track of any changes to these baselines;
- **Quality** – keeping track of how well the deliverables meet predefined quality requirements (technical, functional, aesthetic, and other fit-for-purpose aspects).

Then, once you know what must be monitored and controlled, an analysis of your stakeholders' requirements for progress information will give you an idea of the level of detail required for each dimension. This in turn will guide your choice of how to achieve the required level of monitoring and control and how many persons (with what specific experience, skills and competence attributes) should be allocated to the task/s involved.

Visual progress communication tip: A high-level WBS or PBS can be printed out in a large, readable black-and-white format and then the work package blocks (and/or main deliverables) could be colored in using a RAG status indication (Red, Amber, Green) to indicate progress such as completions and solved/unsolved issues.

Step 8 Control changes (4.3.6)

No project has ever been completed without having undergone changes. Change control is an essential activity in a project. The project manager is responsible for ensuring that each change request is recorded in a Change Register, evaluated and then processed further.

This step is essential because any change can endanger the realization of the project objectives (or even the entire business case). The change request could end up being changed or modified pending the outcome of an impact assessment. The final decision should be communicated to all stakeholders as well as being reflected in all relevant documentation.

The overall impact of a change, together with the substantive impact, is measured against the predetermined project objectives and the business case.

Hints & Tips

'Scope creep' (or the gradual loss of focus on what is supposed to be realized) can be one of the major pitfalls of a project. To prevent this from happening it is important that one starts by preparing a clear plan (of what should be done and when it should be done by). This plan needs to become the scope baseline for the project and can be supported by the creation of the WBS with the deliverables expected from each work package and/or a PBS (Product Breakdown Structure) which only shows the deliverables and not the work involved to create them. Also, the team needs to agree upon rules as to how they should deal with questions about the newly created products, parts that are still not working and need to be replaced, or simply the reparation of faults. In this way all changes follow a process instead of being done without a definite analysis of their impact on the business case.
The process by which one should go about controlling changes should be pre-defined and documented in either an enterprise-wide procedural document or in the Project Management Plan.

Communications tip for change control: To ensure the communication of changes is effective, make sure that your Communications Plan (4.3.38) includes a plan of approach for communicating approved changes. A simple RACI chart can provide a distribution roadmap to ensure that the correct persons are informed of approved changes in a correct and timely fashion.

Changes to items in the Configuration Management system should also be included in this process so that the team is always working with the latest versions of documents.

Step 9 Close the project (4.3.7)

Many projects are started, but it is often forgotten that there should be a clear end to every project as well. Project closure allows the project team to formally verify that the project objectives have been met and to confirm that all work on the project may, therefore, come to an end. In most cases, project closure signifies that the required deliverables have been accepted by the customer and that the project documentation has been archived. This step should also be carried out if a project has ended prematurely.

Hints & Tips

It is good to plan formal project closure at the same time that the Project Management Plan is being put together (i.e. from the start of the project!). This way the project management approach that will be used during the project can also be used as the basis for determining the actions that will be needed to properly close down all administrative, implementation, human resource and financial processes in an efficient and effective manner.

Create a Closure Roadmap as part of the Project Management Plan. Update this roadmap during the course of the project. Continue to add additional actions and update the responsibility matrix associated with the roadmap.

Then, should the project be unexpectedly or prematurely terminated (e.g. due to budget cuts or a change in company priorities) or should the project come to its natural end-point, then no time will need to be expended on figuring out what has to be done to close the project properly.

This way the project team will avoid leaving a mess behind for the organization to clean up when they're gone!

Step 10 Collect lessons learned (4.3.8)

To assist in the effective implementation of future projects, it is important to evaluate the project and to collect and assess both positive and negative experiences. In this way a cycle of quality can be built up within an organization, which in turn will lead to various benefits, (both financial and non-financial). This step ensures that you do not have to re-invent the wheel every time a new project is started up.

Hints & Tips

Ideally, lessons learned from previous projects should be collected and considered at the start of new projects. This often happens sub-consciously at the beginning of programs and projects as project managers 'recall' past experiences prior to starting the project and rely on their personal knowledge of the organization and how to navigate past the

pitfalls inherent within it. The more experienced a project manager is, the better he or she will be at this, but new project managers may need to draw upon these experiences from another source.
It is, therefore, of enormous advantage to the organization, especially for the growth to maturity in project management, if project managers share their lessons learned with the organization. This sharing of knowledge and experiences can greatly improve the organization's overall capability to conduct projects.

Organization: If an organization wishes to derive the most benefit from the experiences gained in each project then it is recommended that they should consider doing the following with respect to projects:

- **Create a central repository for lessons learned** – a long term responsible owner, a means to store and manage received information, and a means to make the stored information accessible to the organization;
- **Make the recording of lessons learned per phase for each and every project mandatory.** If this is not explicitly required from project managers and their teams then the chances are that it will not have the priority and attention to detail that it deserves.

Lessons learned should be seen for what they are: knowledge assets. Assets have value and it is prudent to protect and accrue assets in order to ensure that the value is maintained and increased. A decision should be taken at an appropriate level in the organization to recognize the value of these knowledge assets and to invest in their protection and accrual.

6.3 CASE STUDY: NEW PREMISES FOR PETERSEN & SONS PRINTING COMPANY

This section describes how the principles of the ISO 21500 *Guideline for Project Management* can be implemented through the use of a fictional, practical example.

For the scenario in this case study we opted for a process-driven project in a SME environment to ensure that one could expect the organization to receive a lot of direct leadership from the project manager. We assumed that the organization was already accustomed to working with ISO processes and structures. In this example the ISO 21500 Guideline became the framework for the project and was used as a process description with the emphasis on its use to establish proper *project governance*. It is for this reason that you will come across the various processes in this example, including those mentioned in the Project Roadmap previously discussed in this chapter.

Introduction

Petersen & Sons Printing Company is a healthy medium enterprise, situated on an industrial site at the edge of the city. The printing company specializes in printing for shops and businesses. It employs 75 permanent employees. In addition to the printing department itself, the company also runs a logistics and transport department, a graphic design division (to support customers in the design of layouts of the printed matter and to prepare these for printing), a sales department and a back office.
The company has a highly organized end-to-end business process that ensures orders are processed within record time from order entry in the sales department, via the back office and graphic design to order execution at the printing presses. Subsequently, the printed matter is expediently delivered to the customer by the logistics department.

The organization had no prior experience in running projects, and to date it had never been necessary for them to deviate from the way that they had always done things. Everything that needed to be done in the past could be carried out by the line departments, and the company's business processes were designed such that all customer requests could be resolved using a fixed process. Petersen & Sons is ISO 9001 certified and values process-based working highly.

The Printing Company, however, outgrew the building that they worked in and management decided to move the company to new premises. So they conducted exploratory discussions with the bank and with architects, and eventually they came to the conclusion that the preferred option was to build a new building.

The Board of Directors realized that they would have to deal with many different parties within the project and that the scope of the project would entail many activities with many interdependencies. So they hired a project manager to lead the project. Although the main goal remained the building and furnishing of a new building, the Board also intended to launch more innovative projects in the near future and therefore wanted its employees to become better acquainted with the discipline of project management. So the Board asked the project manager to clearly indicate the process that he would use to set-up, manage and close the project, including how he intended to meet the needs of the stakeholders and how he was going to communicate with them (the Board of Directors) as the primary stakeholder.

Since the company was accustomed to working with ISO processes and structures, the project manager decided to use the ISO 21500 as the basis for his project. He explained to the employees of Petersen & Sons that they should see ISO 21500 as a project management framework with a minimal set of processes and activities that are required in order to execute the project in a correct way. If they ensured that they had a project management process for each of the subject and process groups of the framework, then the project management system would be complete, and they would know what to do and not forget any important steps.

Governance

An important factor in project success is project governance. How will decisions be made within the project? Who has the mandate to make those decisions? Who approves the changes that arise if, for example, something cannot be built as initially planned or is unavoidably delayed? Project governance is often forgotten and tends to only be considered once something goes wrong.

Constructing a new building for the Printing Company is a huge logistical endeavor. The company chose a project method with classic phasing, namely: with a start-up phase, an implementation phase and a closing phase.

The process group classification found in Table 1 of the ISO 21500 (and Table 2.1 of this book) was followed. This table provided useful clues to the task of determining the project's phases.

Initiation

The start of the project went smoothly. A project team was established, consisting of management and more experienced subject matter experts from various departments [4.3.15 Establish the project team], including the architect and the construction company that were responsible for the construction and design of the new building [4.3.9 Identify the stakeholders].

The goal was clear: a new building must be built and furnished. However, to ensure that there were no differences in the interpretation of the project goals, the project manager decided to create a project charter allowing the Board of Directors to state the project goals in their own words [4.3.2 Develop the project charter].

Planning

Due to the fact that building a new property is a huge capital-intensive investment, where errors are difficult and costly to correct, significant time was spent on the planning phase. The requirements and wishes of the users and the details regarding municipal regulations and permits were discussed and tested for feasibility. These activities are often called *Requirements Management* in some project management methods, while in other methods it is referred to as *Scope Definition* [4.3.11 Define scope]. Whatever you choose to call it, it remains important to make sure at the beginning of any project that all aspects of the project are thoroughly considered, and that differences in interpretation are ironed out and everyone involved agrees on the options available and the choices and decisions to be made.

Work soon began on the creation of a work breakdown structure (WBS) [4.3.12 Create work breakdown structure], by decomposing the project into work packages, and by describing the activities in these work packages in detail so that it would be clear to all what was needed to be done [4.3.13 Define the activities]. Project team members were allocated to these activities according to their knowledge and expertise. The dependencies between activities were discussed [4.3.21 Sequence activities] and each person estimated how much time they would need to complete their tasks [4.3.22 Estimate activity durations] and how much each activity would cost [4.3.25 Estimate costs].

ISO 21500 only provides the main points that you have to consider. However, *best practices* that can be used in order to develop a complete plan can be found, for example, in PMI's *Practice Standard for Earned Value Management, Practice Standard for Work Breakdown Structures* and *Practice Standard for Scheduling.*

The project team also looked at the risks involved in the project [4.3.29 Assess risks]. They then looked for subcontractors to perform some of the work packages [4.3.35 Plan procurements, 4.3.36 Select suppliers] and they drew up a communication plan so that both employees as well as customers, neighbors and institutions could be kept informed and involved [4.3.38 Plan communications].

Note: There are two types of project plans that work together to form the total project plan:

1. A *project plan or planning or schedule* that describes **what** should be done and when to deliver the product. For example, the WBS, activities and use of resources.
2. A *project management plan* that describes **how** it should be done. For example, how the project is managed and controlled (reporting, governance, dealing with escalations), how communication is conducted and how risks are dealt with.

When both plans are approved by the relevant stakeholders, then the total project plan is ready [4.3.3 Develop project plans].

Project execution

The time arrived for the construction to begin. The project manager assumed the role of delegated customer and construction supervisor in relation to the chief contractor of the build. Together they directed the daily project work activity [4.3.4 Direct project work] each from his own role's perspective, yet they functioned in unison when reporting to the Board of Directors of the Printing Company [4.3.10 Manage Stakeholders].

During the course of the construction and interior design of the building, it became evident that some of the builders required additional training on the materials being used in the build, and that some employees of the Printing Company still needed to get a quick introduction to the project management processes [4.3.18 Develop the project team]. The project manager, however, had expected this and therefore had sufficient budget and time reserved for training and development of the project team in his project plan.

The project manager also knew that he did not have the technical knowledge to review everything himself, so his plan included the hiring of an architectural consultant who would come on site several times during the project to perform quality assurance [4.3.33 Perform quality assurance] thereby ensuring that the quality requirements were met. And of course when unexpected events occurred that required immediate attention, the project manager was ready and prepared to solve the problems and control the risks [4.3.31 Control risks].

An example of this was when the electricity connection work was suddenly delayed by two weeks and the builder had to be convinced to take on an extra work package after the building was handed over to the customer.

The financial controller of the Printing Company also was actively involved in the risk management processes because of the possible financial and legal consequences of certain risks. ISO 21500 indicates how you can go about risk management in a project but it does not prescribe how one should do it. ISO 21500 however, recommends good practices for risk management. You can also consult the guidelines ISO 31000 *Risk management - Principles and guidelines* (also applicable to projects) and the *Practice Standard for Project Risk Management* from PMI [10].

The project team decided to make an Ishikawa (fishbone) diagram to identify risks [11]. They applied weighting to the risks (probability x impact) in order to prioritize risks in the Risk Register [12] and they determined a plan of action in order to treat the high priority risks [4.3.30 Treat the risks].

Project control
Tight control was maintained on deviations from the original plan [4.3.14 Manage the scope] during the project, as well as on the impact of these deviations on the budgeted time and money. Project progress and expenditure were closely monitored [4.3.24 Manage the schedule] allowing for the comparison of the expected deliverables that had been determined at the creation of the initial WBS and project plans against the realized deliverables to date.

Closure
When the physical building of the new facility was complete and the relevant and current documents and agreements were transferred to the line organization (building management and maintenance), then it was time for a project evaluation. This is when the project team evaluates the project, analyzing the things that went well and those that could have been done better. A final 'lessons learned' session was held in order to record the results of this analysis [4.3.8 Collect lessons learned]. And then last but not least, all bills were paid, all project

documents were archived and the project was formally closed [4.3.7 Close the project phase or project].

Retrospect

For this project, the project team opted for PRINCE2 templates, using the Project Mandate document template as well as those for the Project Initiation Document, the Project Plan and the templates for team roles and responsibilities. They also used the Highlight Report template in which the project manager and the chief contractor documented their weekly progress reports. A monthly meeting was held with the Project Board, which included the executive director of the Printing Company (the 'Executive'), the head of the printing department (the 'Senior User') and the director of the main build contractor (the 'Senior Supplier').

A common conceptual framework

By assigning roles and responsibilities to processes organized on the basis of a common conceptual framework, namely ISO 21500, a common frame of reference for the project management activity was created within the organization. As a consequence everyone interpreted things in the same way and therefore ISO 21500 was successfully implemented in this organization and applied to this project.

7 Future of ISO 21500

7.1 GENERAL EXPECTATION

Ever since the beginning of the development of ISO 21500 in 2007 it became increasingly clear to the stakeholders that an ISO standard for project management would have added value as an overarching standard for existing models, methods and best practices for project management. This awareness set the ball rolling in the project management community and this is still going on. It can already be confirmed that ISO has earned its place within the project management world.

The general expectation is that ISO 21500 will be globally accepted. Perhaps in the long term ISO 21500 will become a key requirement in tenders for large projects in countries or federations across the world. This may reinforce the situation whereby the standard will also be required for smaller contracts.

It is also expected that the project management community will develop specific training offerings, products and consultancy services to support the application of the basic knowledge and best practices of the ISO 21500, in order to further spread the guidance. This may also lead to adaptations and enhancements to the standard in the future. Of course, since ISO 21500 has just been released, there aren't that many best practices around to use. Nevertheless, we expect that these will soon be developed and shared as more and more experience is gained in the practical application of the ISO 21500.

7.2 ADVANCEMENT OF ISO 21500

A standard is never definite. It is merely a record of the norm at a given moment in time. New insights and the application of new and better practices will eventually make it necessary to adapt the standard, to meet the needs of future situations. This will also be the case for ISO 21500. ISO 21500 has been developed as a standard that provides generic high-level guidelines for project management at the organizational level. This means that this version of ISO 21500 is not by definition a reference basis for certification. At the same time organizations are expressing a need for this, in order to have a professional, independent and expert based evaluation of an organization's project management capabilities. For this reason it is likely that the next version of ISO 21500 will develop towards a more prescriptive regime (normative) instead of descriptive (informative) character. When ISO 21500 gains more momentum it is even possible that the existing ISO 10006 *Guidelines for quality management in projects*, dated 2003, may become redundant. Both standards may also be merged, with the result that the differences in approach to quality management in projects, programs and portfolios will have been resolved.

7.3 MOVING TOWARD A FAMILY OF STANDARDS

It is generally recognized that the scope of the project management discipline encompasses far more than what is only covered in the ISO 21500. It is for this reason that it has been decided to continue beyond the scope of ISO 21500, and also look at the development of standards for other aspects in the area of project, program and portfolio management (PPPM).

Figure 7.1 shows how the family of PPPM-standards of ISO relate to each other.

In 2011 the countries that were involved in the development of ISO 21500 have indicated their interest in the specific PPPM topics for which a separate ISO standard could be developed:

- Portfolio management;
- Program management;
- Terminology/glossary;
- Project governance;

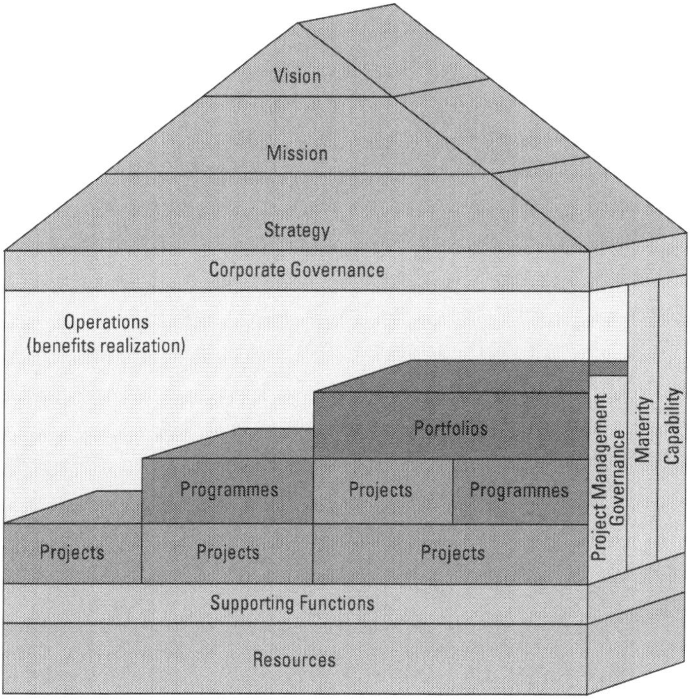

Figure 7.1 The family of PPPM-standards of ISO

- Project management competences;
- Earned value management;
- ISO 21500 maintenance;
- Project management office;
- Personnel competences/capabilities;
- Multi project management;
- Organizational competences;
- Risk;
- Project management maturity;
- Configuration management;
- Change management;
- Portfolio strategy;
- WBS;
- Scheduling;

- Requirements management;
- Complex projects.

The development of new standards with respect to PPPM and the maintenance of ISO 21500 will be governed by the ISO/TC (Technical Committee) 258 'Project, program and portfolio management' which was established in 2011.

Meanwhile, a start has already been made with the drafting of a new standard for 'portfolio management', as well as a study for issuing a standard for 'project governance'. In addition, a proposal has been submitted for the development of a standard for 'terminology for project, program and portfolio management'.

Usually the development of an international standard takes 36 months. At the end, about 16 months are allocated for voting and reviewing and adding comments to ultimately achieve consensus. This may seem very long, but when you consider that different parties from all over the world are involved in this process, and that the aim is to reach consensus, then 36 months is actually quite an acceptable and realistic timeframe.

7.4 MOVING TOWARD A PROJECT MANAGEMENT PROFESSION

The issuing of ISO 21500 is more important than its content may suggest. Its content alone will not create an earthquake in the professional project management world. There is little new under the sun: projects still remain projects and project management is still project management. The significance of ISO 21500, however, goes beyond the content.

The fact that the international professional project management community considers it to be a subject which is important enough to develop a standard for, will definitely be recognized by senior management and their organizations of projects and project management. And rightly so, because we can't think of well-functioning organizations without changes: projects have become an indispensable feature of functional organizations. Projects are also a necessity for innovation. In practice however, project management often has the image of 'that extra little job on the side' and as a result people frequently have relatively little training and competences in project management. Project management is just something you simply do next to your 'real job'.

This has contributed to the perception of project management as not being a 'real' profession, yet this perceived image does not equate to reality. This is partly due to the image created by the project management community itself. From an outsider's perspective it seems to consist of an incoherent maze of terminology and competing standards, methods, models, and best practices, most of which the outside world may not even be aware of. So how can we expect the world to treat project management as a profession if within that profession we still do not agree on what this profession really stands for? The development of one common 'language', one body of knowledge, that clearly defines project, program and portfolio management, the role that projects play in society and the expectations of the project management profession, is crucial for the further professionalization of the profession. For this reason ISO 21500 is an important step on the road to the recognition and acceptance of project management as a 'real' profession.

8 Frequently asked questions and answers

The intention of this chapter is to provide a quick overview of the ISO 21500 Guidance on project management. The chapter contains 100 questions and short answers together with references to additional information in the preceding chapters.

8.1 INTRODUCTION – ABOUT THIS BOOK

1. What is the purpose of this book?
To explain what the new ISO 21500 is all about. See Section 1.1 in this book.

2. What does the guideline imply?
ISO 21500 is an overarching guideline for project management featuring a common framework of knowledge and process definitions for project management. See Chapter 1.

3. What can be achieved with this book?
This book aims to help you gather sufficient insight into the application of the ISO 21500 to be able to apply it in your own project management environmental context. See Section 1.1.

4. What is the audience for this book?
This book is aimed at everyone who works in projects, mandates projects or uses the results of projects. See Section 1.2.

5. How to read/use the book?

The book describes the practical application of the concepts of ISO 21500 in terms of the questions: What, Why and How. See Section 1.3.

8.2 ORIGIN AND STRUCTURE - TRIGGERS

6. What is the economical context?

Billions are being invested in modernizations. Many of these investments are realized by means of projects. See Section 2.1.

7. Why the initiative to create ISO 21500?

The need for the standardization of project management practice led to this initiative. ISO 21500 is a first step in this direction.

8. What are the target audiences for ISO 21500?

Senior managers, customers, project managers, project team members and developers of standards. See Section 2.2.

9. Is this a government initiative?

No, this is an initiative by the international project management community. See Section 2.3.

10. Which countries started up this initiative?

The United Kingdom and the United States of America. See Section 2.3.

11. What were the triggers for the initiative?

The BSI standard for project management was in need of revision. It was decided to replace it with an ISO standard. See Section 2.3.

12. What was the position of the organizations representing the main international standards on project management on this initiative?

PMI and IPMA decided to contribute actively to the development of ISO 21500. There was no significant participation from the UK Cabinet Office (from 1st January 2014 AXELOS, a Joint Venture between UK Government and Capita), who developed PRINCE2. See Section 2.3.1.

13. Does the guideline improve communication?
Yes it can support the improvement of communication within the project environment! It does so by providing a common frame of reference for everyone involved which has commonly understood terms and definitions. These promote mutual understanding and alignment of expectations. See Section 2.3.2.

14. Which sources were used in the formulation of this guideline?
ANSI/PMBOK Guide (by PMI), ICB (by IPMA), PRINCE2, DIN 69901, BS6079, ISO 9001, ISO 10006. See Section 2.3.3.

15. Does the guideline provide a competence profile?
The guideline contains a summary of the ICB competence profile. ISO 21500 indicates the following minimal competences of project staff to enable them to contribute to the project:

- Technical competences, for delivering projects in a structured way;
- Behavioral competences, that refer to the development of personal qualities associated with personal relationships inside the defined boundaries of the project;
- Contextual competences, related to the management of the project both inside the organizational and in the external environment. See Section 2.3.3.

16. How was ISO 21500 developed?
ISO 21500 was developed by means of a multi-stakeholder process, in which experts from all over the world collaborated to define the boundaries of what project management is and is not is about. See Section 2.3.4.

17. Why 21500, why not a different number?
ISO has assigned 21500 to this standard, it being an available number in the series of ISO standards.

18. Will ISO 21500 also be released in languages other than English?
The official languages of ISO are English, French and Russian. ISO 21500 is officially available from ISO in these three languages. In addition to the three official ISO languages, local translations can be made by ISO member organizations in individual countries. For example the standardization organizations of Sweden, the Netherlands and Japan have released local translations of the guideline.

19. What is the purpose of the guideline?

It can be a powerful aid in bridging the differences between the ways that different parties in a project work, thereby enhancing agreement and co-operation between them. See Section 2.3.2.

20. For which types of organizations is ISO 21500 suitable?

ISO 21500 can be applied by any type of organization, including public, private and not-for-profit organizations and for any type of project, irrespective of complexity, size or duration. See Section 2.4.1.

21. How is ISO 21500 structured?

ISO 21500 is structured by subject and area of application. Included are terms and definitions, project management concepts and project management processes. See Section 2.4.2.

22. What information can be found in Chapter 2: Terms and definitions?

Chapter 2 contains some specific project management terms that are not adequately specified elsewhere. See Section 2.4.2.

23. What information can be found in Chapter 3 Project management concepts?

Chapter 3 'Project management concepts' describes ten core concepts that are essential for the execution of projects. See Section 2.4.2.

24. What information is contained in Chapter 4 'Project management processes'?

Chapter 4 'Project management processes' identifies the recommended processes that should be applied to the entire project, or project phase. See Section 2.4.2.

25. What model is applied to ISO 21500?

Five process groups are covered during the project life cycle: Initiating, Planning, Implementing, Controlling and Closing. See Section 2.4.2.

26. Which technique is applied to ISO 21500?

The five process groups are applied according to the Deming cycle (*Plan-Do-Check-Act*). See Section 2.4.2.

27. What is the price of the ISO 21500 Guideline?
The_price of the guideline can be found in the ISO online store (http://www.iso.org/iso/home/store.htm) The guideline is available in both digital (pdf) and printed formats.

8.3 VALUE FOR STAKEHOLDERS - WHY

28. Which countries were involved in the development of ISO 21500?
Over thirty countries were represented in Project Committee PC 236. An exhaustive list can be found in ISO 21500. See Section 2.3.1.

29. What is the general value or benefit of this guideline?
ISO 21500 is an overarching framework for all of the techniques, models and *best practices* of project management. See Section 2.3.1.

30. What is the interest for organizations?
ISO 21500 facilitates the auditing of the practical application of project management techniques and assists in the quality assurance of the project management processes within organizations. See Section 3.2.1.

31. We only do internal projects. What is the added value?
In many internal projects there are external suppliers involved. A guideline like ISO 21500 specifically adds value in managing the interfaces between the organization and external suppliers to ensure proper alignment with external suppliers. See Section 3.2.1.

32. What problem do I solve with it / why should I need the guideline?
This guideline presents a project management model that has the potential to greatly improve and support communication and co-operation between all parties involved in a project. See Section 3.2.2.

33. What is the benefit for a joint venture of (international) organizations?
International enterprises and joint ventures can use the guideline to align parties involved in a project and direct the efforts of international suppliers in an efficient way. See Section 3.2.2.

34. What is the interest for an industry branch or a chain organization?
Industry branches and chain organizations have many members who use differing project management approaches and have their own typical stakeholder types. It is in diverse project management environments such as these that the application of ISO 21500 can add value because it can provide the basis for making clear, mutually understood agreements. See Section 3.2.3.

35. What is the value for specific functional roles within an organization?
In many cases benefits can be achieved when this guideline is applied by everyone in the organization. See Section 3.3.

36. What changes will I notice when ISO 21500 is implemented?
It is quite possible that you may notice no change at all, especially where existing project management approaches are compliant and compatible with ISO 21500, because there would then be no need to make major changes and your organization would carry on as before. The difference will probably be more evident at interfaces between projects using different approaches and in the basis that is used for communication between internal and external project organizations. See Section 3.3.

37. What tools (software) and templates are available?
Tools and templates can be developed using the ISO 21500 process groups as a basis. For example, PMOs can develop these for their own organizations. See Section 3.3.6.

38. What are the benefits for senior management?
The board and senior management can use ISO 21500 to demonstrate that they have their project management processes in place and/or they can use it to improve their project management capabilities. See Section 3.3.1.

39. Are there differences in the application of the guideline between public organizations, private organizations and NGOs?
In general there are no differences, though there may be some differences in the emphasis placed upon certain processes and the measures through which these are applied depending on each project management context. See Section 3.2.2.

40. What is in it for me?
It will enable you to manage projects in a professional way. See Section 3.3.7.

41. What is the benefit for the customer/steering committee?
Customers placing contracts no longer have to prescribe or mandate a specific project management technique when dealing with suppliers just because they are familiar with its definitions. They only have to demand that contractors use the concepts, terms and definitions of ISO 21500. See Section 3.3.2.

42. What are the benefits for quality managers?
ISO 21500 comes from an organization that is internationally renowned for defining and standardizing quality systems for organizations across many industries. It comes as no surprise, therefore, that ISO 21500 places a strong emphasis on quality, whereby the quality of project deliverables can be assured. In this way it takes its place alongside standards for process and product quality, together with providing a basis for an integrated organization-wide quality assurance approach. See Section 3.3.3.

43. What are the benefits for contractors (suppliers)?
The added value for customers/main contractors is that the specification, alignment and delivery of (partial) products can be done in a simple and transparent way, thereby saving both time and money throughout all phases of the project. See Section 3.3.4.

44. Will I become a better project manager by applying the guideline?
If you apply ISO 21500 then it is expected that you will increasingly be better able to operate as a more knowledgeable and effective project manager. Bear in mind, however, that becoming 'better' is dependent not only on knowledge, but also on how the knowledge is used and applied (this is the definition of WISDOM) and, also, that through practice (over time and with continuous use) the knowledge and wisdom will increase the user's level of competence. See Section 3.3.5.

45. Can the guideline be used for certification?
No, since ISO 21500 is a guideline and certification against a guideline is, in principle, not possible. See Sections 3.3.5. and 4.1.

46. What are the benefits for the projects department (PMO)?

The PMO can use the guideline as a basis for setting up an in-house (company specific) set of roles, responsibilities and processes that is independent of project management methods and techniques. ISO 21500 can then be used as a tool to test whether the starting assumptions and chosen approach for projects align with the company's policies regarding roles, responsibilities and processes. See Section 3.3.6.

47. What are the benefits for a project manager?

ISO 21500 supplies the project manager with a benchmark that he can use to check his project plan and project approach for project management completeness and consistency. See Section 3.3.5.

48. Can project managers be certified on ISO 21500?

Not at this point in time; nor is there any indication of the certification of project managers in the future. See Section 3.3.5.

49. What certification possibilities exist for project members?

All of the professional organizations for project managers (APMG, IPMA, PMI) have certification programs for project managers. See the websites of those organizations for more information. See Section 3.3.6.

50. What are the benefits for project team members?

In projects there is always a risk of the project being insufficiently planned and poorly controlled, leading to the project being undertaken in a way that causes problems for the team members, namely too much stress, excessive overtime and in a tense atmosphere. This risk can be mitigated by following the guidelines and principles in ISO 21500 from the start. See Section 3.3.7.

51. Does the guideline contribute to better rules of conduct?

ISO 21500 covers the main requirements for good teamwork and a healthy work environment. The structure promotes disciplined professional conduct. See Section 3.3.7.

52. What are the benefits for a program manager?

The guideline enables the program manager to standardize all projects that are in the program. See Section 3.8.

53. What are the benefits for a portfolio manager?
When developing and applying project portfolio models and solutions, the guideline can serve as a basis for defining the individual projects in a structured way. See Section 3.3.9.

54. What is in it for my customers?
The customer (the end-user of the project result) can be assured that the project manager will use generally accepted principles of sound project management if the project is structured in accordance to the principles and guidelines of ISO 21500. See Section 3.4.

55. Is ISO 21500 applicable to selected types of projects?
ISO 21500 can be used for all types of projects, multi stakeholder projects included. See Section 3.5.

56. Does ISO 21500 make a distinction between different types of projects?
No, ISO 21500 describes the management of projects on a meta level (on a higher level of abstractness) and is therefore applicable to all types of projects. See Section 3.5.

57. What is the value for education and research?
The content of ISO 21500 can provide a sound basis for developing research projects and training programs. See Section 3.6.

8.4 POSITIONING – WHAT, FOR WHOM?

58. What is the core statement of ISO 21500?
ISO 21500 is a global collective reference for project management that leaves one free to choose and apply their own project management method or approach. See Section 4.1.

59. Is ISO 21500 a standard or a guideline?
It is a guideline (or informative standard). See Section 4.1.

60. What does a standard mean?
A standard is a voluntary agreement between interested parties on a product, service, result or process. See Section 4.1.

61. What is the difference between a guideline and a standard?
A standard can be of descriptive (informative) or prescriptive (normative) nature. When talking about a standard we usually refer to a normative standard. When we mean to use an informative norm we usually use the word guideline. See Section 4.1.

62. Does ISO 21500 contain a checklist for a self-declaration?
The guideline does not contain a checklist for conformance to ISO 21500. However, it is possible that someone may develop such a checklist as a prelude to the launch of a future normative edition of ISO 21500. See Section 4.1.

63. Do the existing project management methods converge to form one global guideline?
It is expected that existing project management methods will be measured against ISO 21500 for conformance as time progresses, but individual methods for specific applications will nevertheless remain. See Section 4.1.

64. Does the guideline supply common terms of reference?
Yes, this is the reason for creating this guideline. See Section 4.2.

65. What will ISO 21500 enable us to do in the future what we cannot do now?
It will allow us to cooperate and communicate better in projects because we have a common frame of reference. See Section 4.2.

66. What is the relative position of ISO 21500 to project methods?
ISO 21500 provides globally accepted, common terms of reference for project management in general, which anyone is welcome to use in order to apply to their own method or project management approach. See Section 4.2.

67. Is ISO 21500 a new project management method?
ISO 21500 is not intended as 'another method', rather, it is intended as a collection of globally recognized principles and guidelines with which all project management methods should conform. See Section 4.2.

68. National or global?

ISO 21500 is an independent global guideline for project management that is widely supported all over the world. See Section 4.2.

69. Can ISO 21500 be combined with PRINCE2, Agile, etc.?

Yes, ISO 21500 is a general framework ('what' must be done), as opposed to a method that prescribes 'how' projects can be managed. Project management methods are developed specifically to meet a situational need (technology, industry, delivery requirements, environment, company culture etc.) They provide the details that you need and that fit nicely within the framework that ISO 21500 provides. So you can use your choice of project management methods within the generic project management framework (ISO 21500) to ensure that the completeness of your project management approach is not compromised by your need for method flexibility. See Section 4.2.

70. Is this guideline intended for a quality office (like ISO 9001)?

There are many points of process overlap between ISO 21500 and ISO 9001 (quality management systems), however the difference between the two is that the latter is specifically aimed at assuring the quality of the project result whereas the former is concerned with the quality of the project management processes leading to the realization of the project result. If you only use ISO 21500 in your project then you may have top quality project execution but with no quality guarantee for the project result. See Section 4.3.

71. What is the risk if I don't use ISO 21500?

When the principles and framework of ISO 21500 are not used as a basis for communication and for expectations management in a project, then the risk of miscommunication due to a mismatch in processes and deliverables, and decreased synchronicity becomes increasingly possible. These factors will make co-operation with other stakeholders more difficult and increase the company's chances of losing potential customers, especially when these customers require compliance or compatibility with international standards. See Section 4.3.

72. Can we combine ISO 21500 and CMMI?

Yes! ISO 21500 provides a process management structure and project management best practices (for better management of a project) whereas CMMI provides a process management structure and systems and software engineering best practices (for better engineering of systems and software). When they are combined then the addition of the ISO 21500 project management processes to the CMMI management processes will result in better and more complete project management of systems and software engineering projects. See Section 4.4.

73. How does it relate to organizational maturity?
One thing that is common to all concepts defining organizational maturity and the resultant maturity models is that it has a clear, transparent managed process and understandable terminology (a common language). ISO 21500 presents both and is therefore a good basis for moving towards project management maturity. See Section 4.4.

74. How were the professional associations involved?
An employee of PMI Headquarters (USA) served as secretary for PC 236 and a representative from Germany of IPMA participated as an observer. Also several active experts were sponsored by local chapters of IPMA and PMI. See Section 4.5.

75. What does PMI think of the ISO 21500?
The PMI organization was an active contributor to the development process of ISO 21500 and PMI acknowledges ISO 21500 as a global project management standard. The latest (fifth) edition of the *PMBOK Guide* is aligned with ISO 21500. See Section 4.5.

76. What does IPMA think of the ISO 21500?
IPMA was also an active contributor in the development of ISO 21500. IPMA did not release a formal reaction to the release of ISO 21500, but several member organizations reacted positively to the guideline. It should be expected that in the development of the ICB version 4, IPMA will align its terminology to the concepts and glossary as described in ISO 21500. See Section 4.5.

8.5 IMPLEMENTATION AND APPLICATION- HOW, BY WHOM?

77. How should I prepare for the implementation of ISO 21500?
When implementing ISO 21500 a decision has to be taken to apply the guideline:

a. As the basis for the execution of project management;

b. As the basis for performing quality reviews (as in a maturity model);
c. To design project management processes and their interfaces with the rest of the organization.

See Section 5.1.

78. Before the start: what will I need to do?
The first steps of a project are in the Initiation process group and cover getting an authorized project charter, the composition of the project team and the identification of project stakeholders. See Section 6.1.

79. How can I implement ISO 21500?
The guideline contains many detailed steps (processes) that together constitute the basis for setting up a project. See Section 5.1.

80. Do I need help in implementing ISO 21500 or can I do it myself?
You can either implement ISO 21500 yourself or use external training and consultancy services. It is expected that the market will provide these training and consultancy offerings soon. See Sections 5.1, 6.1 and 7.1.

81. What are the steps to complete the implementation of ISO 21500?
The final steps of a project are in the Closing process group and consist of the formal closure of the project (depending on the method used for archiving), financial closure, getting discharged by the steering group and the collection and dissemination of lessons learned. See Section 6.1.

82. When is the implementation finished?
When the Closing process group is completed and all relevant documents have been produced. See Section 6.1.

8.6 FUTURE – THE NEXT STEPS

83. Will best practices for ISO 21500 become available?
ISO 21500 contains *best practices* for project management. *Best practices* on how to use ISO 21500 are not yet available, because it is a new guideline. Once experience with ISO 21500 has been established, it is likely these best practices will become available.

84. Will manuals be published?
This book provides answers on the most frequently asked questions about ISO 21500. There are ideas about a handy summary, for example a *pocket guide*. IPMA and some national standards committees will consider further publications on ISO 21500.

85. Are references to ISO 21500 yet available?
Yes, on the Internet are several blogs and forums on ISO 21500. Also on LinkedIn two ISO 21500 groups exist.

86. Where can I find the latest news on ISO 21500?
Information of ISO 21500 and the development of other ISO standards can be found on the ISO's website (www.iso.org).

87. Are ISO 21500 training courses and products available yet?
Not yet, however it is expected that the market will develop a range of trainings services. See Section 6.1.

88. Where can I get advice on the implementation of the guideline?
Once the guideline is used more widely, then a large supply of consultancy offerings can be expected. See Section 6.1.

89. Can ISO 21500 become mandatory for RFPs for tenders?
This will be the case if certain countries or the European Committee decide to stipulate ISO 21500. It is likely to be used for future tenders for large projects. See Section 7.1.

90. Why is ISO 21500 a guideline and not a standard?
In principle ISO 21500 has been developed as a guideline, being informative and consultative in nature, which describes what project management is on an organizational level. ISO 21500 is of a descriptive nature (and therefore a guideline) and not of a prescriptive nature. At this time that is the highest attainable nature. See Section 4.1.

91. Will ISO 21500 ever become a standard?
ISO standards and guideline are periodically reviewed. The benefit of a standard is that certification against it is possible. ISO21500 was developed as a guideline.

Some voices in the market say that there is a need for certification of the design and organization of project management on an organizational level. Therefore it is possible that the next edition of ISO 21500 will be more of a prescriptive (normative) nature instead of descriptive (informative). See Section 7.2.

92. Are there alternatives for organizations that want to demonstrate that their project approach conforms to ISO 21500?

In the Netherlands a pilot is being prepared for a self-declaration of conformity to ISO 21500. There are no known comparable initiatives (yet) in other countries. See Section 4.1.

93. Will ISO 21500 replace ISO 10006?

As ISO 21500 gains popularity, it is possible that the old ISO 10006 'Guidelines for quality management in projects' that dates back to 2003 will be discontinued. See Section 7.2.

94. What next?

It is generally accepted that the discipline of project management covers more than just the content of guideline ISO 21500. Therefore it was decided not to stop with the development of ISO 21500, but to look further and, where needed and possible, come to agreements on other aspects of project management, like program- and portfolio management (PPPM). See Section 6.3.

95. Is PC 236 involved in future developments?

No, PC 236 has been discontinued. A new Technical Committee (TC 258) has been created that is tasked with the development of the next version of ISO 21500 and also the development of new standards in the areas of project- program- and portfolio management. See Section 7.3.

96. Is there a relationship between ISO 21500 and governance?

Governance is the framework for managing organizations. The subjects of project governance cover areas of corporate governance that are specifically associated with project activities. The TC 258 study group Project Governance will define the interfaces with project programs and portfolios. See Section 7.3.

97. What will come after ISO 21500?

The countries that were involved in the development of ISO 21500 have identified and prioritized the subjects they are interested in. The result of that process can be read in Section 6.3 of this book.

98. What is the timeline for future standards on project management?

The development of two new standards has already begun: one for portfolio management and one for project governance. Interest has also been expressed in starting the development of a standard for project-, program- portfolio management terminology. Since the development of a standard can take up to 36 months and as this development is based on volunteer work by the stakeholders, the TC 258 Work Group will coordinate the work for the next few years. See Section 7.3.

8.7 ATTACHMENTS – MORE INFORMATION

99. How can I contribute to the development of ISO standards?

Please refer to your national standardization organization (ISO member organization) for information on how you can participate in the development of international standards.

100. Who have participated in the writing and editing of this book?

This book was originally written by 17 Dutch members of PC 236 and members of the Dutch ISO 21500 Interest Group (comprising representatives of the Dutch chapters of IPMA and PMI). See Annex D.

Annex A About ISO

ISO (International Organization for Standardization) is the world's largest developer of voluntary international standards. ISO consists of a network of national standards bodies. These national standards bodies from all over the globe make up the ISO membership and they represent ISO in their country.

Key principles in standard development are openness, transparency, the involvement of all stakeholders and a consensus-based approach. Stakeholders can participate in the standards development process via their national standards committees. They are then able to vote and comment on drafts of standards and/or participate in the technical committees of ISO that create standards.

Here are the mission statement and objectives of ISO [13]:

ISO mission statement:
'The mission of ISO is to promote the development of standardization and related activities in the world with a view to facilitating the international exchange of goods and services, and to developing cooperation in the spheres of intellectual, scientific, technological and economic activity.'

ISO objectives:
- *'Conformity assessment' means checking that products, materials, services, systems, processes or people measure up to the specifications of a relevant standard or specification. Today, many products require testing for conformity with specifications or compliance with safety, or other regulations before they can be put on many markets. ISO guides and standards for conformity assessment*

represent an international consensus on best practice. Their use contributes to the consistency of conformity assessment worldwide and so facilitates trade.

- *'Certification': there exist many testing laboratories and certification bodies which offer independent conformity assessment services.*

Annex B Terms and definitions of ISO 21500

Chapter 2 'Terms and definitions' of ISO 21500 contains sixteen specific definitions of project management terms. Here are these definitions. Other project management terms that are used are sufficiently defined in other chapters of the guideline, in the ISO-list of definitions[14] or in the Oxford Dictionary.

	term	definition
2.1	**activity**	identified component of work within a schedule that is required to be undertaken to complete a project.
2.2	**application area**	category of projects that generally have a common focus related to a product, customer, or sector.
2.3	**baseline**	reference basis for comparison against which project performance is monitored and controlled.
2.4	**change request**	documentation that defines a proposed alteration to the project.
2.5	**configuration management**	application of procedures to control, correlate, and maintain documentation, specifications and physical attributes.
2.6	**control**	comparison of actual performance with planned performance, analyzing variances, and taking appropriate corrective and preventive action as needed.
2.7	**corrective action**	direction and activity for modifying the performance of work to bring performance in line with the plan.
2.8	**critical path**	sequence of activities that determine the earliest possible completion date for the project or phase.
2.9	**lag**	attribute applied to a logical relationship to delay the start or end of an activity.
2.10	**lead**	attribute applied to a logical relationship to advance the start or end of an activity.
2.11	**preventive action**	direction and activity for modifying the work to avoid or reduce potential deviations in performance from the plan.
2.12	**project life cycle**	defined set of phases from the start to the end of the project.

	term	definition
2.13	**risk register**	record of identified risks including results of analysis and planned responses.
2.14	**stakeholder**	person, group or organization that has interest in or can affect, be affected by, or perceive themselves to be affected by any aspect of the project.
2.15	**tender**	document in the form of an offer or statement of bid to supply a product, service, or result, usually in response to an invitation or request.
2.16	**work breakdown structure dictionary**	document that describes each component in the work breakdown structure.

Annex C References

[1] Advanced Economies Investment (% of GDP) Statistics, *http://www.economywatch.com/economic-statistics/Advanced-Economies/Investment_Percentage_of_GDP/.* 2012.

[2] Project Management Methodologies, Useful Information from Prolific Bloggers, *http://infolific.com/technology/methodologies/.*

[3] ICB-IPMA Competence Baseline, Version 3.0, IPMA, *www.ipma.ch*, 2006.

[4] PRINCE2, *www.prince-officialsite.com*, 2012.

[5] A Guide to the Project Management Body of Knowledge (*PMBOK® Guide*), 5th edition, Project Management Institute, *www.pmi.org*, 2013.

[6] ISO survey 2010.

[7] Zelfverklaring ISO 26000 voor MVO, *www.nen.nl/iso26000*, 2012.

[8] John P. Kotter, Leading Change, ISBN 9780875847474, Harvard Business School Publishing, 2008.

[9] Practice Standard for Project Risk Management, Project Management Institute, *www.pmi.org*, 2012.

[10] Practice Standard for Earned Value Management, Practice Standard for Work Breakdown Structures and Practice Standard for Scheduling, Project Management Institute, *www.pmi.org*, 2012.

[11] PRINCE2 for Dummies 2nd edition, Nick Graham. Wiley & Sons, chapter 15 Managing project risk, 2010.

[12] Risk register, *http://en.wikipedia.org/wiki/Risk_register*, 2012.

[13] ISO-vision and objectives, ISO-website, *http://www.iso.org/iso/support/faqs/faqs_ conformity_assessment_and_certification.ht*, 2012.

[14] ISO Online Browsing Platform provides you with easy access to ISO standards, graphical symbols, codes or terms and definitions, *www.iso.org/obp/*, 2012.
[15] ISO 21500:2012 Guidance on Project Management, ISO, *http://www.iso.org/iso/catalogue_detail.htm?csnumber=50003*, 2012.

Annex D About the authors, editors and translators

This is a book about and by the industry. The first edition (in Dutch) was jointly written by seventeen authors and based on their project management experience and knowledge. This translation was initiated as a result of international interest for the publication in English, for the international community. Depending on further interest, translations in other languages may follow.

André Legerman, Anton Zandhuis, Gilbert Silvius, Rochelle Röber and Rommert Stellingwerf edited the book and translated it into English. André Legerman was the project manager of this English edition.

The editors and translators of this book:

André Legerman: PMI certified Project Manager (PMP) and Program Manager (PgMP). Active internationally for more than thirty years as a project/program manager and project delivery manager. Consultant for project turnarounds, professionalization of project organizations and assessments and coaching of project managers. **André** was president of PMI Netherlands Chapter and a member of the Netherlands standards committee ISO 21500.

Anton Zandhuis: internationally recognized consultant, trainer and coach at Threon, European specialist in practical project management best practices for consulting, training and tooling. Anton is co-founder and director of the PMI Netherlands Chapter, (co-) author of various publications, including 'A pocket companion to PMI's *PMBOK Guide*' and the English edition of the *PMBOK Guide*, and EMEA representative on the PMI Management Advisory Group the Registered Education Providers. Anton is enthusiastic, pragmatic, results-oriented and driven to continuously improve the knowledge and discipline within the project area.

Gilbert Silvius: Principal Consultant at Van Aetsveld change and project management, and independent academic with affiliations at universities in the Netherlands, Belgium, United Kingdom, Austria, Vietnam and South Africa. Gilbert is the initiator and program lead of the first Master of Project Management in the Netherlands. In research, he focuses on the integration of sustainability in project management, a topic on which he has also published several books.

Rochelle Röber PMP: certified as a CAPM and PMP planner, project manager, PMO consultant and project management coach. Rochelle has experience in and knowledge of different project management frameworks and techniques including *PMBOK Guide*, TOC, Agile DSDM, Scrum and PRINCE2. She has worked on projects in various sectors, including telecommunications, banking and financial services, ICT projects and vehicle construction. Rochelle's current specialization is planning and scheduling in various project management approaches.

Rommert Stellingwerf: PMI certified Project Manager (PMP). Independent project management professional and Owner-director of Staversk BV. Thirty years of international experience in IT and projects at Shell. Rommert was a member of the board of PMI Netherlands Chapter for several years. He is active in developing ISO standards for project, program and portfolio management. He participated in the development of ISO 21500 and is co-author of 'ISO 21500 – A Pocket Guide'. Currently he is Convener (Chairman) of the ISO TC/258 study/ working group on Governance of projects, programmes and portfolios.

About the authors of the first (Dutch) edition of this book:
To assess the usability and impact of ISO 21500 for the Dutch market, PMI Netherlands Chapter (PMI-NL) and IPMA-NL jointly founded the 'ISO 21500 Interest Group' with Dutch experts in December 2009. The members of the standards committee and the Interest Group are very active and enthusiastic about ISO 21500: they have translated the guideline after its publication in Dutch and are actively promoting the guideline in The Netherlands, together with PMI-NL and IPMA-NL. These members of the 'ISO 21500 Interest Group'

wrote the first Dutch edition of this book as part of the awareness effort and to encourage use of the guideline itself.

Andre Legerman and Rommert Stellingwerf edited the Dutch edition. Anton Zandhuis was the project manager of the Dutch publication. The other authors were: Ad Heijmans, Ben Bolland, Erik Scholten, Frans Soelman, Gerda Nijp-Bosma, Gilbert Silvius, Maarten Peelen, Marcel Mars, Pieter van der Knaap, Robbert van Alen, Rochelle Röber, Ron J. Vinken, Sander van der Blij and Stefan van Aalst.

20196495R00059

Printed in Great Britain
by Amazon